Creating a Better Relationship
with Your Money, Yourself, and Others

Reframing

RICH

STEVE COUGHRAN

WITH JESSICA MEEHAN

RIVER GROVE
BOOKS

Published by River Grove Books
Austin, TX
www.rivergrovebooks.com

Distributed by River Grove Books

Design and composition by Greenleaf Book Group
Cover design by Greenleaf Book Group
Cover images used under license from
©Adobestock.com/HiSunnySky

Publisher's Cataloging-in-Publication data is available.

Paperback ISBN: 978-1-966629-52-8

Hardcvoer ISBN: 979-8-88645-148-1

eBook ISBN: 979-8-88645-149-8

First Edition

First and foremost, this book is dedicated to God, who continuously bestows upon me His abundant grace, showers me with tender mercies, and empowers me to make a positive impact on people's lives worldwide. Secondly, I dedicate this to my beloved family that serves as my unwavering support system and constant source of motivation. Lastly, I extend my heartfelt gratitude to the incredible community members who continually inspire me with their unwavering ambition, insatiable curiosity, and boundless kindness—I hold each and every one of you in deep affection.

Contents

Preface: The Lowest Place on Earth   vii

Introduction   1

PART I: GETTING YOUR MINDSET RIGHT

Chapter 1: Starting with Self-Awareness   11

Chapter 2: Your Relationship with Money   21

Chapter 3: The Power of Reframing   31

Chapter 4: Obstacles to Your Path of Abundance   43

Chapter 5: Letting Go to Get What You Want   53

PART II: BECOMING FINANCIALLY FIT

Chapter 6: Six Drivers of Financial Fitness   63

Chapter 7: Planning   67

Chapter 8: Earning   85

Chapter 9: Spending   99

Chapter 10: Borrowing   105

Chapter 11: Investing   115

Chapter 12: Giving   125

PART III: CHANGING YOUR RELATIONSHIPS WITH MONEY

Chapter 13: Money and Relationships   133

Chapter 14: Making Other People Feel Valued   159

PART IV: TAKING ACTION

Chapter 15: The Missing Component of the
Laws of Attraction and Vibration   177

Chapter 16: Increasing Your Capacity to Receive   195

Chapter 17: Working On Your Relationship with Yourself   207

Chapter 18: Asking Better Questions   221

Chapter 19: Harnessing a Mindset of Abundance   231

Notes   247

About the Author   251

The Lowest Place on Earth

The day was finally here. As I stared out the window of our tour bus, I felt a surge of anticipation for what was to come. The trip had been planned more than two years earlier, but it had been pushed back several times, interrupted and postponed by the "messy" parts of life. The parts you don't usually plan for, the totally unexpected. Now this trip was as much a vacation as it was a mission to heal myself. I wondered if the stories I'd heard about this place were true. Would I really float? Did the water's minerals hold the key to fixing the parts of me that were broken? Was it that simple? Looking back, it was a time in my life when I had a lot of questions, and I hoped this place would have the answers to some of them. And it did. When we finally came to a stop, I stepped off the bus with cautious optimism and took in my surroundings. I couldn't believe it. I was actually here. I could taste the salt in the air, smell the sulfur as it wafted off the water. And although this was my first time visiting the Dead Sea, in a way I'd found myself there before—at "the lowest place on Earth."

Don't get me wrong, I know life is full of ups and downs, and I have been blessed with some very high highs in my forty-odd cycles around the sun. Having said that, I've also had to overcome a number of extremely low lows, some of which I felt like I'd never rise up from. In retrospect, I could have seen some of the lows coming. I grew up with an absent father who struggled with substance abuse for years before finally leaving us for good, followed by a number of ill-equipped stepfathers who were neither suited for nor interested in being a role model for me and my six siblings. At a very impressionable age, I found that my self-worth was linked to how other people treated me. I was acutely aware of the fact that people kept leaving me, and I felt like they didn't think I was worth sticking around for, like I wasn't valuable. When I was sixteen years old, I left home with no money and no idea how to start or run a business. I felt vulnerable, but I was on a mission to prove that I mattered. I believed that if I could prove to people that I was valuable, they wouldn't leave.

Getting married was a high, and getting divorced fifteen years and two kids later was, unequivocally, the lowest low point in my life. Combined with all the personal and professional devastation that came with the COVID-19 pandemic, my decoupling brought to light the massive void I had been trying to mask with my ambition and excessive drive to achieve. Without the distraction of work and travel, I was left feeling broken and worthless again.

To answer your anticipated question, yes, I *did* float in the warm and salty sea. And the feeling of weightlessness was one I welcomed. Until that moment, I hadn't realized how heavy the things I'd been holding on to had become, or how much I'd let them weigh me down. But being in the waters of the Dead Sea showed me how good it could feel to let go of that stuff for a moment and just float.

Earlier that year, I'd hit rock bottom. Not from drugs or alcohol, but from a pure identity/life crisis. For some people, the COVID-19 pandemic was a welcomed opportunity to slow down, take advantage of the work-from-home culture, and connect with loved ones. It offered many people time to look inward and reflect on where they were in their lives, but for me, it brought the fast-paced lifestyle to which I'd grown accustomed to a grinding halt.

In the years leading up to the pandemic, I was thriving. On the business side of things, my energy was heavily focused on growing my consulting firm and finding new ways to expand that business; earning my MBA from Duke University's Fuqua School of Business; writing my second book, *Outsizing*; traveling multiple times per month; and working seventy hours a week helping companies turn themselves around and grow. I was thinking and planning and moving nonstop because, frankly, I was fixated on being productive.

I was high on life, and I loved how accomplished I felt from a business perspective, but in addition to these professional obligations, I was dedicated to my personal responsibilities too. In my private life, I was raising two amazing kids, serving in a leadership role in my church, and training to run my sixth marathon.

I was always busy, but if I'm being honest, I was sort of stuck in a revolving door of avoidance when it came to my marriage—constantly moving but not really getting anywhere. My marriage had been on the rocks for years, and by that point, it was *toxic*. Despite knowing that, I was reluctant to leave because I thought that would make me exactly like my dad, and I didn't want that. I couldn't bear to disappoint my kids the same way I'd been disappointed, but I had to be honest with myself—it was time to leave.

When the pandemic started, all the professional and personal things that kept me busy were suddenly out of reach. I went from sitting in boardrooms to sitting in my room, bored. And the longer I sat, the harder it became to ignore the things I'd been neglecting. The opportunity to escape into my next client's project or take an impromptu trip just wasn't there anymore, and I knew I was going to self-destruct if I didn't change my mindset. I had to tackle my problems head-on, feel the pain, embrace it, accept it, and let it go . . . but at the time, I wasn't sure exactly how to do any of that or where to start.

Feeling weightless now reminded me that negativity in any form can weigh you down if you hold on to it for long enough. In the months that had preceded this trip, I had been holding on to a lot— pain, anger, and disappointment. But those emotions had been slowly dissipating and were now being washed away with every lap of the waters against my skin.

As the salt from the warm waters kept my body afloat, I put my head back and tried to let my mind drift. Despite being thousands of miles away from my home, the things that I'd been holding on to still seemed to be right there beside me whenever I closed my eyes. Even though I felt more at peace than I had in months, I couldn't help but reflect on how dramatically different my life had been just several months earlier.

Cards on the table, I know I wasn't a perfect partner, but I had been miserable for years. I want to be clear, though, that I take full responsibility for the role I played in my marriage ultimately failing, and I can honestly say I only want the best for the mother of my children. The decision to get a divorce wasn't a choice I made lightly, however.

Throughout my life, I've found that being in or near water has given me the space to be alone with my own thoughts. Perhaps that's why I ended up at the Dead Sea. For a long time, though, my shower has served as my sanctuary to reflect and introspect. There,

I receive most of my inspiration and clarity on my thoughts, and the day that I decided to leave my marriage was no exception. The water was hot, but my skin, like the rest of my body, was numb. I didn't *feel* anything, physically or emotionally. The sound of the shower was loud enough to drown out the anxious voice that had been taunting me whenever I found a moment of stillness. I let the water wash over me, focusing on the feeling of every drop hitting my body, and then my mind went quiet. As I stood there, a small whisper broke the silence: "She cannot hurt you anymore." That was it. One simple phrase that gave me the permission I needed to move forward and become free. It was at that moment that I accepted the decision to move on, because I understood that if I didn't, this marriage was going to destroy me and my ability to be there for the people I loved. And although coming to that decision took a huge weight off my shoulders, the hard part was what happened in the months that followed.

I'm a very deep feeler, so when I get hit with the big emotions, it takes a toll on my body physically too. Our divorce wasn't finalized for another ten months, during which time I felt the effects of being spread too thin. I was still working on expanding my business, trying to build a new home for my kids, navigating difficult negotiations with lawyers, racking up legal bills, and attempting to stave off the depression that consumed me a little bit more each day. I didn't want to be sad, struggling Steve anymore; I wanted to be Super Steve again. I wanted to give my time and passion to the things that brought me joy (my God, my family, my *life*!).

What we resist persists, I reminded myself. And so, I gave myself a deadline to pull myself together and get back on my feet. As part of that effort, I gifted myself the trip to the Dead Sea. It may seem random, but setting a deadline is a strategy that previously worked for me. Right before I turned twenty, I found myself at a low point.

I was struggling with my closest relationship and losing weight from the emotional toll. Overall, I lacked purpose, to the point that the future felt hopeless. I decided to give myself ninety days to get my life in order. I told myself that during that period, I would let go of all the pain I was holding, start working out, and look for new hobbies. Having that deadline in front of me worked. I pulled myself out of my precarious state, put some muscle back on, and picked up cycling. I even went back to university and made some great new friends.

Now, being submerged in the potentially powerful waters of the Dead Sea was the catalyst I needed for my next complete physical and mental transformation. This time, beyond the obvious things I had to do, such as finalize my divorce, build a new home, and turn my company around, my strategy was to pursue a new mindset, one that prioritized purpose and passion over simply being productive.

I was curious to see what powers the mud of the Dead Sea held, so I dug my fingernails into the silty clay and smeared a thick layer over my forearm. There, in that moment, I felt like a broken man, and I desperately wanted to fix myself. Briefly, I contemplated what it would be like to cover my entire body with that clay. What if I could build myself a clay cocoon and emerge a new, changed man? A *healed* man. I wanted to float in those calm, serene waters forever, but I'd have to get out eventually, and I hoped I would be able to leave all of the emotional baggage there when I left. I mulled it over as I floated around at about 420 meters (about 1,300 feet) below sea level, and then it suddenly dawned on me. No matter how much of this miracle mud I covered myself with, I couldn't heal myself from the outside. I suddenly felt as heavy as a stone, filled with trepidation at the thought of just how much changing I had to do. But I had done it before. I'd picked myself up from other lows, and this would be no different. I just needed a foolproof strategy.

Introduction

Leading a successful life is a lot like running a successful business; having a solid strategy is imperative for both. Sure, ambition and resources are important, but without a plan, an idea will never get further than the drawing board. And even if it does, it's essential to have a strategy that evolves, both with the company itself and the ever-changing environment of the broader business market. The first thing I learned about having a business strategy was the importance of understanding the language of money, because financial illiteracy can and does ruin people's lives.

When I refer to financial literacy, I'm not talking about becoming some numbers nerd who wears the stereotypical green accounting shade and performs debits, credits, and other mathematical equations related to money all day. Instead, to be financially literate goes beyond just understanding numbers and financial concepts; it also involves grasping the story behind those numbers. It requires the ability to interpret financial information, analyze trends, and make informed decisions based on that analysis. Being financially literate empowers individuals to take control of their financial lives and make sound choices that align with their goals.

But I certainly had no idea about financial literacy when I was younger—and I later learned some hard lessons as a result.

When I left home at sixteen, I moved in with my middle sister, Nadine, and her husband. They were just starting out and trying to raise young kids, so, like many new families, money was tight. They let me move into their basement, and I repaid them by helping out with household chores and chipping in for groceries whenever I was able. Financial scarcity was definitely a reality for all of us, though. Between the three of us, we had virtually no savings, and despite making sacrifices on things where we could, our expenses were almost as high as our combined income. With little more than an idea and a whole lot of blind faith, I started my first business out of my sister's garage; it evolved from installing sprinklers into a landscaping company.

Growing my first business was definitely a high point in my life at the time, but it also led me to a significant low: *failing* at my first business. I was so focused on increasing our client base, hiring new team members, and fulfilling new projects that I neglected the company's broader financial fitness. As a result, a lot of employees had to face unnecessary suffering. I had to let people go and be accountable to the fact that my own bad strategy had ruined people's lives. Knowing I was the reason for so many others' hardship was a very low moment for me.

Lightbulb Moment: If you own, or plan to own, a business, financial literacy can help prepare you for change in two ways: First, it allows you to think beyond what your company is doing now and gets you thinking about a plan for how you can expand your business and increase its value. Second, it primes you with the tools you need to respond to difficult, unpredictable changes in the broader business market, like a pandemic or a volatile economy. You don't need to own or run a business to benefit from financial literacy skills, though. In fact, being financially literate can improve your financial preparedness for changes in your personal life, too, including marriage, kids, unemployment, disease, divorce, and death. Financial literacy gives you the skills to know how to plan for and cope with these changes so you can minimize the negative impact they might have on you financially.

When I started my business, I wasn't thinking long-term or about financial fitness. I genuinely didn't have an understanding of the "running the business" side of running a business. I knew my own worth, and I knew the value of the work I was doing, but at the same time, I projected the beliefs I had about my own scarcity onto my customers. You see, in my mind, because I didn't have money, I didn't think people could afford to pay me thousands of dollars for high-end renovations to their yards. The beliefs I held in my mind about financial scarcity led me to thinking small, charging less, and struggling to make any meaningful profit. Instead of charging people what I knew the job would cost (and factoring my own profits into the cost), I wound up cutting into my own profits out of fear that my customers would think the price was too high and pull out of the project altogether. Eventually, I became tired of not making any profit and realized that if I charged people what the jobs were *worth* and didn't disadvantage myself by trying to cut costs by limiting my own profits, I'd be able to buy more equipment, expand my services, and build a bigger, better business. Over the next twelve years, with the help of my brother who eventually joined me, my business grew into an office of more than forty employees. I was proud of myself, and I was grateful for my brother. It felt like I had things figured out, but in reality I still had a lot to learn.

It wasn't that I believed we were "too big to fail"; it was that I didn't anticipate the things that would lead to our eventual failure. To put it another way, it wasn't arrogance but *ignorance* that was the ultimate Achilles' heel of my first business. I can still remember how my stomach churned with anxiety as I walked into the boardroom filled with employees I was about to let go. It was in December 2009, right before Christmas. All week, employees had been jovially sharing their plans for the upcoming holiday, blissfully unaware of the unfortunate news I'd been carrying around with me for months. I stood in the conference room, looking at the faces of the people I'd hired—some employees had been there since day one. These individuals had dedicated their time and effort over the better part of the last decade to helping my business succeed.

"I'm sorry," I said, a lump rising in my throat, "but I can no longer keep you on as employees." I watched as their faces shifted from confusion, to fear, to anger. I felt ashamed. How could I call myself a leader after what I'd let happen to my own company? It wasn't just the failing company I suddenly had on my hands that worried me; it was the lives of the people I had effectively ruined, all because I had been using an undeveloped business strategy.

That day, I vowed to never let another bad strategy negatively impact other people's lives again. I made a promise to myself to become a better leader, to learn the ins and outs of effective business strategies, and most importantly, to share my knowledge with others to help them avoid the mistakes I'd made that had cost my employees their jobs. Looking back, I made three critical mistakes that, had I avoided, I probably wouldn't have had to give up on my first business. My first mistake was not understanding the language of money. I'm embarrassed to admit it, but I didn't even know how to read a financial statement, let alone use one to help my business thrive. Second, I approached my business with a mindset of scarcity rather than abundance. That mindset played a big part in choosing to play it safe with my business. I had grown comfortable with the ease of securing new jobs from the extended economic boom and expanding new construction market. Projects were easy to come by, so I gave up opportunities to grow and expand into other landscape services that would benefit the company during times when new construction contracts became few and far between. Last but not least, I didn't have a strategy that enabled me or my business to adapt to change. A myopic business vision meant that not only was the company blindsided by changes we didn't see coming, but we also weren't equipped to deal with them.

Overcoming these three mistakes became the backbone of the work I did over the next decade. I committed myself to studying, researching, writing, and consulting on others' business strategies to help leaders transform their companies, improve performance, and above all else, avoid making the same mistakes I did. Fast-forward over a decade later, I was turning around and growing other companies with my own successful business strategy consulting firm. I was no longer thinking small or letting a mindset of financial scarcity get in the way of realizing my bigger purpose. My mission now is to elevate businesses by empowering people with an understanding of the fundamentals of strategy and finance to power growth, innovation, and resilience to reach their full potential.

Having said that, let me be clear: I'm okay with the fact that I failed. In fact, I'm glad I did, and I take full responsibility for the failures I've faced, because they have been an important part of learning how to succeed and being able to teach others to do the same. And I'm still learning. There's always work to be done because the inevitability of things is that, just as sure as there will be more highs for us to celebrate, there will almost certainly be more lows to dig ourselves out of. Failing doesn't mean giving up, though. Failing has taught me a valuable lesson: If we don't hold ourselves accountable for the things that happen in our lives, we allow ourselves to be the victims of our failures. When we take responsibility for our failures, whether in business or in our personal lives, we are reminding ourselves that we *are* in control and empowering ourselves to change.

Which brings me to the purpose of this book. This book is not a "get-rich-quick" guide (believe me, the only person getting rich from those is the one selling them to you). It is also not a Band-Aid strategy to fix a business that doesn't have the right foundation to thrive. (It's okay if that's where you're at, but also recognize there is work to be done beyond reading this book.) I hope this book will be a practical blueprint to success, financially and beyond. I know that everyone walks a different path in their life, and my path isn't necessarily the one that will suit everyone best, but I want to teach you the steps I have personally taken over and over again to pick myself up and rebuild my business—and more important, my *life*. I've had to transform my mindset and grapple with some soul-searching questions to figure out what my true values are and how I can live a life that honors those values. I want this book to be a tool that inspires you to do the same.

Throughout this book, there will be moments when I ask you to reflect on a key point or try an exercise that has helped me to recenter myself. Or I may ask you to simply think about where you are, where you want to go, and how you can get there. I ask that you keep an open mind, dig deep, and be honest with yourself when it comes to answering the big questions. And regardless of whether you're just starting out as an entrepreneur or you're well past retirement, it's never too late (or too early) to transform your business (and your life) into one of abundance. I encourage you to not only learn to recognize the tools for transformation, but to truly take advantage of them to build a successful strategy for business and life.

The truth is that transforming anything is difficult. It requires us to work hard, to attempt and embrace trial and error. To succeed is to struggle, but that doesn't mean you should have to fail in the same ways I did. Learn from me, learn from my mistakes, and then use this wisdom to change your own life permanently. It all starts with understanding your mindset when it comes to finance. I don't just mean thinking about money, but rather thinking about *how* you think about money.

PART I

Getting Your Mindset Right

CHAPTER 1

Starting with Self-Awareness

Developing the right mindset about an area of your life (whether that's financial, social, occupational, etc.) means gaining a better understanding of your thoughts, feelings, beliefs, and attitudes. Understanding these key parts of your mindset can be beneficial because they improve things like self-control, decision-making skills, and self-awareness. Perhaps more crucially, understanding your own mindset enables you to identify and manage limiting beliefs and emotions, learn how to be resilient, and cultivate a growth mindset. Strengthening your mindset starts with being more self-aware. Too often, we allow ourselves to merely go through the motions of our routine, running on autopilot with the other eight billion people who share this planet with us. When we're wrapped up in our day-to-day tasks, it's easy to take our place in life for granted.

Lightbulb Moment: Think about your place in life. What is the one thing you can do differently today to change the direction of your life tomorrow? Now, take a moment to think about what you do on a day-to-day basis. What daily patterns are helping you get closer to that goal? Are there any daily patterns that are perhaps keeping you from reaching that goal? If our daily patterns don't align with the bigger goal, it will be very difficult to get there. We can't get healthy by snacking on junk food, we can't become a great entrepreneur by sleeping in late every day, and we can't become financially fit by practicing unhealthy spending habits. The impact of one small change can ripple into abundant success. Whatever it may be, just remember, it's the small things that usually make the biggest difference.

Your place in life

Consider where you are in life right now. Are you fresh out of college? Middle-aged? Retired? What country do you live in? Do you live in a city or the suburbs, and who do you live with? Do you love what you do for a living? Now, think about how your place in life differs from the rest of the world. At the end of 2022, the number of people living without electricity totaled 775 million—that's about 13 percent of the global population.[1] The number of people who still don't have access to clean, safe water is nearly double the US population. From a socio-political perspective, roughly one-third of the people in the world live in nations that aren't "free," gripped by oppression, corruption, and human rights discrimination. Let's compare finances: In the United States, the median annual income is around $70,900 per year. If you earn more than $50,000 a year, you're joined by more than half the population that makes up the middle class. How does this compare to the rest of the world? Globally, Monaco has the highest annual income per capita at just over $186,000, compared to Afghanistan, where the annual income per person is a fraction of a percent of that at just $390 annually.[2] The statistics are overwhelming; I get it, but that's kind of my point. Without the awareness of where and how we live compared to other people around the world, we lose our ability to manifest an attitude of gratitude for what we *do* have.

When we take our place in the world for granted, we ignore the fundamental truth that where, when, and how we come into existence is meant to help us become who we are destined to be. There's only a 4.2 percent chance of a person being born in the United States. That chance gets even smaller for being born to middle- or upper-middle-class US citizens. Warren Buffett calls this the "ovarian lottery," which conceptualizes the profound idea that you were born at a specific time, in a specific place, with your specific identity rather than being someone else, somewhere else, at some other time. Although Buffett is the one who popularized the term, the original concept comes from the mind of John Rawls, a brilliant Harvard philosopher and author of the book *A Theory of Justice*.[3] The premise suggests that if you have access to things like water, electricity, food, safe housing, education, and financial resources, you've won the ovarian lottery. It's easy to feel entitled about where we were born, how much money our parents have, where we go to school, our earning potential, and even who we become friends with, work with, and marry, but the reality couldn't be further from this. I believe that all life is a gift and nobody should ever mistakenly assume they are better than someone else simply because they are better off than them financially. So why do we consume ourselves with thoughts about what we *don't* have or how we feel we've lost the ovarian lottery? Sometimes it's because we lack gratitude for our place in life.

My Grandma Sylvia grew up in Idaho in the late 1930s. Her family was never well-off; in fact, she spent the first twenty-five years of her life with no electricity or indoor plumbing. She got married and started her own family, but their collective income was minimal. Living off the land they owned meant long hours of hard, physical labor and often only just enough to make ends meet. But every mouth was fed, and every face was happy. She never mentioned poverty or scarcity and never uttered a despondent word about what she lacked. She always said she had an abundant life and was fully content with the life she had lived. To me, she is the epitome of someone with an attitude of gratitude.

While having a positive attitude can help shape the way we interpret our experiences, I do want to recognize that sometimes people can be victims of circumstance. Misfortune can befall anyone, and during that time, it's okay to have a few tough days or even a few very tough days. It doesn't matter if you aren't perfectly positive all the time; what matters is that you're able to recognize (even on those tough days) the blessings that you do have in your life. I'm not perfect at being positive, but I have learned to exercise gratitude, and I want to give you the tools to do the same so you can shift your focus on those tough days and be empowered to change your circumstances wherever possible.

I had my own reckoning with the ovarian lottery while I was visiting New Delhi, India, as part of my MBA program at Duke University. Without a doubt, this is the moment I go back to when I'm asked about when or how my financial mindset changed. To set the scene, it was 2016, and I was on a bus headed for one of India's most densely populated areas in the country, downtown New Delhi. Before we were able to get off the bus, our driver turned to us with a word of caution: "For your own safety, don't give *anyone* any money." The implication was that if we gave money to one person, we'd quickly become a spectacle and subsequently be taken advantage of.

Cautious of his warning, I was half a dozen steps from the bus when I realized just how serious our driver had been. Downtown New Delhi is a sensory overload; it's a place that looks vast and open yet seems to overflow with people. It's got the hustle and bustle of sellers and buyers but is equally populated with people who aren't equipped to do either. I saw school-aged children walking around unaccompanied with little else to do but stand and beg. The majority of people around me were wearing old, dirty-looking clothes and, despite a lack of paved walkways, most were barefoot. The air was dusty and filled with the smell of exhaust fumes, which lingered due to how hot and dry the climate is. It was rampant poverty if I'd ever seen it. To put things in perspective, India has a mean income of just over two thousand dollars per year, an amount that is simply unlivable in the United States.[4]

Compared to these locals, my life back in the United States was beyond luxury. As I walked through the downtown area, reflecting on just how different my life was from this reality, a little girl stepped into the street about thirty feet ahead of me. She looked to be around six years old (three years older than my daughter at the time) and was carrying what looked like an old cloth bag over her shoulder. As she walked toward me, feet bare, clothes ragged, my heart sank as I realized that what I'd assumed to be a tattered bag was in fact her baby brother, draped like a towel over her shoulder. She stopped a few feet away from me, and I looked down to meet her gaze. Her face was a blank stare, but she had piercing yellow-brown eyes that were filled with despair as she extended an open, empty hand. She pointed to her mouth and then touched her brother's back.

Sorrowfully, and I cannot stress that enough, I turned away as our bus driver had advised. I felt absolutely devastated. I could feel the weight of inequality, and it shook me to my core, but I also felt a renewed sense of gratitude for my own place in life. I had never gone a day without electricity or water, and I'd never been without food or clothes either . . . compared to her, I'd won the lottery!

Walking away from those kids was the hardest thing I've ever done. I felt guilty and angry and helpless—but it also gave me a new sense of purpose and fueled a new drive to do more good in the world. Looking back, that was *the* moment I felt the pull to be an influence for good and bless the lives of people with the resources that I've been gifted. And so there, some eight thousand miles away from my home, I promised myself I would use every opportunity I was given in life to reach beyond and inspire others to elevate themselves. And by that I mean I was committed to taking financial responsibility in my life and using more of my resources to bless the lives of others. Not just financially, though. The pain I felt for those kids in that moment was the spark that fueled my greatest mission—a mission to help others understand financial literacy, learn how to become financially fit, and be empowered to be an influence for good in the lives of those around them. I knew I couldn't save everyone, but I knew I could do better to help others do better for themselves so they could ultimately become what they were destined to be. We are all financial stewards of the money we receive in life. How we use it is up to us, and it's often determined by our place in life. If we maintain the perspective of how our place in life compares to those around us, we can apply a mindset of gratitude to our life and our finances.

Your financial place in life

Now that you've spent some time thinking about your current place in life, let's consider what your current *financial situation* is. Where are you financially? Do you *own* your home? Your car? Do you owe more money in debts than you have in savings? Do you have a 401(k) retirement plan? Are you currently running from creditors or behind on bills? Take a minute to be really honest with yourself about your financial place in life. Are you someone who feels secure and comfortable about their finances, or are you anxious and fearful about the amount of money you have? If you're the first type of person, great, but you probably know there's still a lot to learn.

And if you're the second type of person, you're not alone. I've been there. Coming from a family with zero disposable income, I spent most of my young life focusing on trying to squirrel away as much money as I could. Then one day, after fifteen years of marriage, my wife and I got divorced, and we split our assets. After I'd spent the last decade building wealth and securing my financial freedom, I was left with half of my entire life savings. I had to rebuild myself and my finances and start over in a lot of ways.

The bottom line is that it doesn't matter where you are financially—rich, poor, in debt, or overflowing with money—wherever you are in your life, I will meet you there, without judgments. We're going to evaluate your financial place in life to find out where you want to be and walk this journey together until you get there!

✓ CHECK YOURSELF

The skills you have can determine whether your trajectory toward financial freedom is a clear path or one that is boobytrapped with obstacles. How you get to where you want to be in life all depends on your trajectory. Think of your trajectory as where your intentions and your actions align. We can have the best of intentions, but if we fail to

continued

act in accordance with them, we'll never get anywhere. And that applies to all areas of life. With that in mind, think about a goal you have. It can be anything, from running a marathon to earning a million dollars! Now, ask yourself: Do my daily patterns match my goal? Is there something you can change about your daily patterns that would adjust your trajectory to better meet that goal?

I've worked with a lot of people to help them get on the right trajectory to meet their financial goals and beyond, and I know from these experiences that where many people get stuck is on their income earning capabilities. Yes, some people do spend frivolously or rack up huge amounts of debt, but often what I see is more of an *earning* issue than a spending problem. Consider the goal you used in the Check Yourself exercise. Does your current skill set allow you to achieve that goal? What type of jobs are you capable of doing with those skills, and where is there room to grow moving forward? Sometimes it's necessary to pursue learning opportunities in the near term that will set you on the right trajectory in the long run.

Another common mistake people end up making is stealing from their future selves. No, I don't mean an older version of you is going to jump out, Terminator-style, and question you about where all their money has gone, but how we spend money now will determine how we spend it in the future. Let's get something straight: Some debt is *not* optional. The vast majority of people will incur some kind of long-term debt for a necessary purchase they couldn't ordinarily afford (like a house or a car), but that's not the debt I'm talking about. In reality, your future self is on the hook for any unnecessary debt you rack up now. If we're wise about our earning and spending, we can make sure that future you isn't mad at current you for spending so nonchalantly. The truth is that clothes, cars, and technology all go out of style eventually, but saving for your future self will never *not* be the trendy thing to do.

Why is saving money and then investing it so crucial? Well, being financially accountable is essential for your current and future selves. It will allow you to save in the short term so you can use that money later if and when you need to. Maybe it feels like a grind right now, but in the long run you'll be better off saving up any disposable income you have than if you'd invested in material things. For example, when I was thirty-one years old, I hated my job. And I wasn't alone; my colleagues hated their jobs, too. Where we differed, though, was that I had six months of my mortgage paid in advance, while they continued living paycheck to paycheck. It wasn't that they spent frivolously; life is seriously expensive. Rather, it was because I was hypercautious about where my money went. I would always make sure I was sacrificing or putting off whatever I could in order to save and invest. Unlike them, I had the freedom to quit overnight, knowing that I'd still be able to live off the money I had accumulated. Saving in the short term literally bought future Steve the financial freedom to change his life. It's hard to predict exactly when an emergency or sudden change in your financial circumstance will happen, but if you get real with yourself now about whether your spending patterns are essential or frivolous, you can evaluate those patterns and save money in case your future self needs it (and I guarantee your future self will).

🧠 Exercise Your Knowledge

Write down three things current you values that money can buy:

1. _____

2. _____

3. _____

Now, imagine yourself thirty years older. What does your life look like? Are you retired? Are you still living paycheck to paycheck? Consider whether the three things you wrote down would still be valuable to future you. Would buying them have been a help or a hindrance to the trajectory you wanted to be on?

Now, imagine yourself another fifteen years older. What does your life look like now? If you had saved your money rather than spending it on material gains in the short term, would you be better or worse off?

Here's the take-home message: When we have gratitude for our place in life and we understand what our goals are, we can figure out the best trajectory to ensure that our intentions and our actions align. To do that, we need to be financially accountable and recognize how patterns in our day-to-day life are either enabling or preventing us from achieving our higher goals. Being financially accountable means having a better grasp over the finances you can control (like necessary versus unnecessary debt) and knowing how and when to save and invest. When we have savings, we feel more secure, and it's this security that empowers us to do bold things and take risks. It gives us the confidence to pursue other opportunities, take different jobs, and learn new things. When we're empowered, we fear less, and being fearless opens us up to abundant opportunities.

CHAPTER 2

Your Relationship with Money

What is your definition of financial abundance? Maybe it's having a six-figure savings account or enough money to buy a second (or third) home. Perhaps it's having just enough to pay your bills each month and keep your debt to a minimum. Whatever it means to you, the mindset you have when it comes to money does matter, because that will influence the strategy you use to earn it and the choices you make when it comes time to spend it.

Sometimes, though, how we spend our money isn't up to us. In today's world, there are certain nonnegotiables we must spend money on like food, housing, transportation, and other necessities of life. If we're able to, we might put some of what's left into an investment fund or spend it on leisure activities. Beyond those things, emergency expenses can happen—a visit to the emergency room, a necessary but expensive car or home repair—or you could experience a severe business downturn due to circumstances outside your control. And your mindset will be key in how you deal with those major financial setbacks.

> **Lightbulb Moment:** Financial setbacks are, like death and taxes, another certainty in life. At some stage of your life, in some way, shape, or form, you will incur an obstacle that sets you back financially. Change will always come. Expect it. Accept it. Sometimes change comes like a wave, and if you can't ride it out and adapt, you're going to drown trying to resist it. I had to remind myself once, so now I'm reminding you: What you resist *will* persist.

Facing financial setbacks

In 2009, during the height of the financial crisis, a friend of mine shared a story that shocked me to my core. She told me about a friend of hers who was completely consumed by their business. They were incredibly productive, but it had gotten to the point where every thought they had and every choice they made was for the business. Even around their community, the business was synonymous with their name because they were so deeply invested in making it a success. They were the business, and the business was them.

I'm not saying that's the wrong way to do things, because running a great business does take up a majority of your time, especially when you're still setting up and getting established. However, this particular person, who sacrificed relationships and time to put all they had into their business, ended up losing everything during the financial crash. Having their identity so closely tied to their business meant that once their business was gone, they no longer knew who they were. They had few meaningful relationships left because they were fixated on securing the financial side of their business, and at the end of the day, losing the business became a major setback in their life, one they simply felt like there was no coming back from. I'm sorry to say that, unfortunately, this story doesn't have a happy ending. Tragically, that friend ended up taking their own life. I'm not saying this to be macabre or to scare you away from investing time and resources into your own business, but rather to provide a cautionary tale to remind you that there's more to life than just business and money.

This person's story isn't a lesson in vain ambition (because it's important to be ambitious); instead, it serves as a reminder that if you prioritize financial abundance over having a life of abundance in terms of the quality of your relationships, you may end up losing a large amount of both. I experienced the same thing during my divorce. At the time, I felt cheated, as though all the sacrifices I'd made didn't mean anything because I'd fallen short of the life I was working so hard for and ended up giving half of it away. In hindsight, I had a mindset of "I came from nothing, and I've done this all by myself, so this isn't fair." In reality, that's just how divorce works. The rules are there to be equitable but evidently are not always equal. Regardless, at the end of the day, what I gave up in my divorce was insignificant to what I gained in having to rebuild my mindset. I had the opportunity to pick myself up, reassess my mindset (including when it came to my finances), and build a happier, more fulfilling life.

> ### ✓ CHECK YOURSELF
>
> Write down what money means to you. It can be as literal or metaphorical as you want, but spend some time reflecting on your relationship to the word *money*. Ask yourself, If I had unlimited money, what would I do with it? Who or what would I spend it on?

Avoiding the scarcity mindset

You may have heard the expression "Money can't buy you happiness, but it's more comfortable to cry in a Ferrari than on a bicycle." In 2010, Nobel Prize–winning psychologist Daniel Kahneman published a study that would change the way people think about their own lives.[1] In his research, he found that, beyond an annual income of around $75,000, money had a significantly smaller effect on how satisfied a person was with their life. Years later, even after adjusting for inflation, happiness levels do plateau after a certain amount, and people who earn double that aren't twice as happy.

Why am I telling you all of this? The study results might seem pointless, but I think they're really profound, because they demonstrate that having a mindset of abundance doesn't start and end with finances. I'm not pretending that wealth inequality isn't real. It is very real, and it's beginning to drive a serious wedge in the distribution of well-being among people on a global scale. *Why?* Well, if everybody had equal access to an abundance of resources, then we'd have no such thing as "classes," and there would be no power that governments and companies could wield over their citizens and consumers.

Particularly in the United States, we live in a consumer-driven society, with more than 70 percent of our gross domestic product coming from consumption. A huge part of that consumption is that we are conditioned—often unknowingly—into believing that we will only be happy if we buy that bigger house, fancier car, or newest fashion item. In believing this, we fall into a trap of constantly being unsatisfied, desiring more than we have, and ultimately delaying our happiness. The truth is, with that mindset, enough will never be enough. Pride is a pervasive part of the human experience. It presents itself through excess, vanity, and gluttony because the alternative is simply too terrifying to consider: scarcity. The good news is that it doesn't *need* to be that way. We can train ourselves out of that scarcity mindset and use it to our advantage.

From a young age, I was instilled with ideas and beliefs that fostered a scarcity mindset. In financial terms, I grew up poor, but I was rich in the values of family, health, faith, and friendship. Unfortunately, values don't pay the bills, and that was obvious to me as I watched my mom exhaust herself working two jobs just to make ends meet. It was also obvious to me when I left home at the age of sixteen and had to figure things out for myself. Looking back, I wasn't scared, or even aware, of the business obstacles I needed to watch out for, because I was operating with the intention of just having enough money to cover the basics, like paying my rent. Not living paycheck to paycheck didn't even register with me as a possibility, because I was trapped in a scarcity mindset. I told myself I was a victim of circumstance and had no control over how things worked out. More than that, I believed that if I didn't have enough money, then *I* wasn't enough, and that's a destructive thought to operate from.

The dogma that "money is the goal" is counterproductive. Here's why: When we establish a desire for something (tangible or otherwise), we are subconsciously reminding ourselves that we don't have it. We desire what we lack, and when we fixate on what we don't have, we create a mindset that is driven by fear and scarcity. In and of itself, that mindset then becomes an obstacle to achieving the thing we desire.

On the flip side, when we grapple with what money means to us and let go of the feeling of lack, we allow money to become subservient to what we truly desire. If we want more respect, self-worth, and freedom, we can get there a lot faster without the need for money. Instead, if we work on developing attributes of kindness, compassion, empathy, love, and faith, these will earn us self-respect a lot faster than money will. Money just becomes a resource to help us achieve our highest, most fulfilling purpose.

For me, money now means that I have the freedom to do what I'm truly passionate about. That means connecting with people like you, being a positive influence in your life, and helping you take back the power when it comes to your finances. I've never been someone who likes to be told what to do or how I should live my life, so having enough money to be able to cover essential expenses, provide a secure lifestyle for my kids, and use the rest to focus on achieving these higher goals is my financial sweet spot.

When I started out, like so many people, I was constantly chasing money, because money *does* matter. Having money is essential to surviving, and having more of it means it's easier to adapt to sudden changes and fix unexpected problems. What I'm getting at, though, is that if we focus on simply achieving financial abundance as a means to generate more wealth than we need to overcome problems in our lives, we will never be satisfied. We can achieve financial satisfaction when we have the means to bless our lives and the lives of others. Believe me, I know hundreds of people who have enough money to last for ten lifetimes, and the truth is that quite a few of them are miserable and unfulfilled.

By fixating on money as the end goal, we are giving in to the most insecure part of ourselves, the part that makes us feel small and embarrassed that we don't have the things we desire. These feelings condition us to use money to compensate for these insecurities. Here's the catch: The more we try to use money to satisfy our smaller self, the more money we'll need to satisfy those inner feelings of smallness. So, how do we break this cycle? Well, if we can address the source of those feelings and focus our mindset on what we truly desire, money no longer becomes the end goal. Instead, we can learn to view money as a tool to help us achieve bigger, more meaningful goals. When we identify what our higher goals are, the need to gratify our smaller self with money becomes unnecessary, and when that happens, we start to adopt a mindset of financial abundance.

As I've gotten older—and I like to think *wiser*—I've realized the things that have added the most value to my life aren't the things that cost the most money. As I mentioned earlier, in today's society, we are conditioned into consumerism and taught to believe the most valuable things are the things that have the biggest price tag. At the end of the day, I like to think that we are all just souls placed on earth through the ovarian lottery. That's not to say that where we end up is random, though. To me, we have all been given the opportunity to exist, however briefly, on the earth side of the universe to grow and find our purpose. I believe the things that matter the most are the things that money can't buy: connecting with people, fulfilling our passions, laughing with the people we love. Money satisfies our ego, and yes, we do need it to survive, but I want you to think beyond being "rich" and consider the other possibilities that financial abundance can give you that will satisfy your soul, too.

A mindset of financial abundance does more than just stifle our feelings of smallness. It allows us to let go of the anxiety and despair that comes from trying and failing to satisfy those feelings with money. Remember, in life we manifest what we subconsciously tell ourselves we deserve. Therefore, if we limit ourselves with a negative belief system focused on lack and deprivation, that will be the reality we ultimately experience. We might accept a lower socioeconomic status because that's what we believe we deserve. If we have a scarcity mindset, we may settle for that position, and then there may never be enough money to get ahead and achieve financial freedom.

That's why it's crucial to adopt the mindset that we are filled with unlimited potential, that we are capable of achieving an abundance of things. Having a mindset of financial abundance encourages us to think about money as a resource to bless our lives and the lives of those around us. It allows us to be in control of our money and how we use it, rather than letting the money control us. When money controls us, it often leads to negative attributes like vanity, arrogance, and jealousy, which simply cannot exist in the presence of other feelings like true fulfillment, gratitude, and completion.

True financial abundance means that money becomes a resource to satisfy ourselves, rather than an object of satisfaction. And by satisfying ourselves, I don't mean spending all the money on *stuff*. Satisfaction can come from using our position of financial abundance as a resource to bless the lives of others. In doing this, we can satisfy our own soul and obtain an even higher level of fulfillment. When we find ways to satisfy ourselves and allow ourselves to let go of a scarcity mindset, we create the opportunity for abundance to come into our lives. You've probably heard the expression "seeing the glass as half empty," and it makes sense for someone with a scarcity mindset to view the glass that way. In an abundance mindset, though, it isn't just about seeing the glass as half full; it's about filling up the glass with an abundance of the *right* stuff: passion, connection, appreciation, contentment, and giving. I want to show you how to become a "glass-runneth-over" person, and it starts with setting intentions and then letting them go. Believe me, I'm not always perfect at keeping an abundant mindset, but I've learned a lot about how valuable letting go of a scarcity mindset can be.

Exercise Your Knowledge

Our early experiences with money have a significant impact on our mindset and behaviors when it comes to how we approach our finances as adults.

Write down your earliest experience with money. Was it given to you as a gift? Did your parents open a savings account for you? Did you have to earn it on your own?

Now, consider the following questions:

- Did you spend that money or save it?
- Did this experience with money have an influence on how you currently view money?
- How is your mindset on finances now similar or different to your mindset when you were younger?

Reflecting on your early experiences with money may help you understand your current attitudes and behaviors when it comes to money, including how and when you choose to spend it. Being aware of this influence can help you develop smart, safe relationships with money.

CHAPTER 3

The Power of Reframing

Prentice Mulford famously wrote that "thoughts are things."[1] Mulford was one of the philosophers that pioneered the New Thought movement, which suggests that the cause of all human suffering (whether physical or emotional) is the effect of incorrect ways of thinking. Now, I am a man of faith, but I also believe wholeheartedly in modern medicine and the idea that disease and illness have etiologies and cures beyond "it's all in your head." Having said that, this movement does encourage people to think more deeply about the power of their thoughts and the impact they can have on their day-to-day lives.

> **Lightbulb Moment:** How we think, feel, and behave are all intricately connected. Spend a moment trying to wrap your head around just how remarkably interconnected our

continued

thoughts, feelings, and behaviors truly are—and the profound impact they can have on our psychology.

Simply put, what we think affects how we feel and behave, which in turn affects how we subsequently think, feel, and behave. Don't be discouraged if you need to read this section over again a few times. The thoughts-feelings-behaviors relationship is an incredibly complex tri-directional phenomenon, but let's break it down together.

Let's say you're about to go for an important job interview. Depending on your mindset, you'll likely behave differently because of the way your thoughts, feelings, and behaviors all interact. If you approach the interview with a negative mindset, you might think things like *I'm not good enough for this job* or *I'm never going to get this job*. If you think that way, you're inclined to feel more anxious or stressed as well as unprepared. During that interview, your behavior is going to reflect those feelings, and you might appear nervous, make mistakes, or find it difficult to answer questions confidently.

Alternatively, you could approach the interview with a positive mindset, a mindset of *abundance*. Having an abundant mindset means shifting your focus away from any insecurities about what you lack or where your limitations are and toward the plethora of possible opportunities that lie ahead of you. When you approach crucial moments like this with a mindset of abundance, you might find yourself thinking, *I am qualified for this job, and I have the skills and experience they're looking for* or *I'm going to be myself and do my best*. Internally, these thoughts might cause you to feel more confident and more engaged, leading you to behave that way in the interview and come off as a good fit for the position.

This simple example shows the interaction, both positive and negative, between thoughts, feelings, and behaviors; the power of an abundance-oriented mindset; and how, in combination with an abundance-oriented mindset, the interaction of your own thoughts, feelings, and behaviors can be the keys to harnessing success.

✓ **CHECK YOURSELF**

The next time you find yourself overwhelmed by a feeling, try this exercise. Close your eyes and take a deep breath in through you nose and exhale through your mouth. Notice how you're feeling and try to put a label on it. Tell yourself: "I'm feeling ___." Take another breath in and out. Then, tell yourself: "I'm noticing that I'm feeling ___." Take a third breath in and out and tell yourself: "I'm thinking about noticing that I'm feeling ___." This exercise is designed to create distance between you and your feelings. By zooming out, we remind ourselves that we are not our feelings. By allowing ourselves to simply become an observer of our feelings, we actually reduce our emotional responses.

Reframing your thoughts

Although thoughts are temporary, if we allow them to, they can lead to permanent changes in the way we feel and behave. Thoughts don't occur inside a vacuum; they can pop in and out of our stream of consciousness at any time. One fleeting feeling can produce a thousand related thoughts, which is why they're so impossible to control. If we work on changing our feelings by learning to reappraise them in a nonthreatening way, we can stop the negative train of thought in its tracks.

When we practice accepting our feelings rather than avoiding them, we can learn to become indifferent to the feelings we have and allow them to simply appear and then disappear, along with the thousands of associated thoughts that come with them. This will allow us to feel differently, behave differently, and eventually *think* differently. If we do this consistently enough, over time our mindset changes, too. This is known as cognitive reframing.

In simple terms, cognitive reframing is a psychological technique that involves identifying, and more importantly, *modifying* negative or unhelpful beliefs, thought patterns, or interpretations. If we don't address these thinking patterns, they can lead to long-term, maladaptive behaviors. As I mentioned earlier, our thoughts are virtually impossible to control, and sometimes they pop into our head "automatically." And because we have very little control over them, these thoughts are often irrational or biased and can have a negative influence over how we feel and behave. Thankfully, cognitive reframing works by encouraging us to challenge these types of thoughts and consider alternative, more realistic explanations.

So, what about thoughts that aren't transient? Those thoughts are a little more difficult to reframe because they are often embedded in our way of thinking from a young age. Unlike fleeting thoughts, mental scripts are learned through our childhood experiences and carried into adulthood. For example, when my dad left, my siblings and I had to learn to navigate the world without a father figure. Fortunately, my mother, who is simply an incredible woman, was there to give me the love and support I needed to thrive. However, because she had six other children to provide for, I had to figure out a lot for myself. Now, hindsight is twenty/twenty, and in retrospect, being independent from a young age was an incredible blessing, but when I left home at sixteen, I carried this do-it-yourself mental script with me. I believed that everything was up to me—that I was the only person I needed to make things happen. For a while, relying on my own strengths worked, but as you can imagine, pretty soon this mentality caught up with me, and I ended up burned out, anxious, and isolated. It was a humbling lesson, but a necessary one. I came to realize that I needed to learn how to accept help from others and lean on the collective power of those around me. Moreover, I discovered the importance of placing my trust in something *bigger* than me—a higher power, beyond my capabilities.

These mental scripts can include things like biases and stereotypes that we encounter over our lifetime that get encoded into our thinking processes. Often, these are feelings we haven't zoomed out from, so they play a pivotal role in how we think, feel, and behave.

Now, how does this all relate to having a mindset of financial abundance? Well, financial scripts are a type of mental script we've programmed into ourselves over time. To get a sense of what your financial scripts might be, consider what your current perceptions about money are at this moment in your life. Maybe you believe Wall Street is full of swindlers or all rich people are narcissists. Maybe you feel like wealth is generational and it's impossible to make money unless you have money to spend on a great business idea. Perhaps you're keenly aware that there is rampant global poverty and you think there will never be enough money. Thoughts like these have been gradually coded into your financial mental script over time and have shaped your experiences with money.

Our thoughts are the code, and what we experience in our lives are the projections of that code, manifested through our behaviors. Here, *behavior* broadly means the choices we make and how we *act*. This might include choosing to engage in certain behaviors, like investing, strategizing, associating with particular social groups, and even taking up specific hobbies. Together, these behaviors shape our reality. This can be very empowering, but it's easy to see how a faulty code or mental script can have negative consequences on our reality.

To reshape our reality, we need to teach ourselves a new code, a new way of thinking, starting with challenging our unconscious biases.

Biases can be preferences or prejudices we have against specific people, things, or actions. Often, we don't even know we hold a bias toward something until we catch ourselves acting on it. You might think, *Geez, I'm a horrible person for thinking or doing* ___, but the truth is, biases are a very useful part of our evolution.

Particularly, unconscious biases can help us take mental shortcuts to fill in the blanks wherever possible. Think about it—even just as you're reading this sentence, your brain is trying to process about 11 million other pieces of incoming information. You could be worrying about a work deadline, or all of your responsibilities piling up at home, or a fight you had with your partner last night, or a new passion project you've started, or that friend you've been planning to catch up with, or the workout you keep putting off, or the bills you've been meaning to pay, or all the student debt you have to pay back or . . . *all those things at once!* Frankly, it would be impossible to function if we couldn't take shortcuts.

Sometimes, though, our unconscious biases negatively impact our behavior when these thoughts guide our actions. We aren't born with these prejudices coded into our mental scripts, but we can acquire negative associations through other people and experiences at a young age that get coded into our behavior as we grow up. It could be a throwaway comment you heard when you were younger like "If homeless people weren't so lazy, they'd go out and get a job so they could afford a house." Unknowingly, a comment like that might influence how you interact with this group of people in later life.

Similarly, if your mental script is encoded with the belief that Wall Street and the stock market is all a sham to help rich people get richer, you may be inclined to behave in accordance with that script.

You may choose to not put any money in any stocks and miss out on a huge investment opportunity.

Overcoming unconscious bias doesn't happen overnight. It's a conscious, iterative process that starts with increasing our awareness of and ability to recognize when and how we act on our biases. By digging deeper into the root cause of our biased thinking, we can then apply what we know about reframing to change how we feel and act. *Boom!* Granted, it took me almost two decades to really understand this concept and learn how to apply it to my own life, but let me tell you, reframing has played an enormous role in rewriting my mental script to one of abundance, and it can do the same for you.

✓ CHECK YOURSELF

This exercise is designed to get you thinking about reframing by using a personal example. Think of an experience you've had where a situation or person made you feel really upset or hurt. Keep this experience in mind as you read over the steps for reframing your thoughts.

Step 1. Describe the situation. Try to recall what you were feeling during the experience (anger, fear, sadness, resentment, etc.). Also try to recall what you were *thinking* at the time.

Step 2. Write down six alternative ways you could interpret the situation differently from the way you described it above.

Step 3. Refer to the way you initially described the situation and ask yourself the follow questions:

- Is my story true?

- Does my story align with my personal values?

- Does my interpretation of the story give me the power to act?

continued

When you take a step back from the situation itself (and the immediate thoughts and feelings that come with it), you give yourself the capability to consider how you want to interpret what's happening and make an informed decision about how to respond. It's important to honestly ask yourself: Am I acting on an unconscious bias? Am I truly a victim in this situation, or am I deceiving myself?

Think about what your personal values are (kindness, grace, empathy, etc.) and then ask yourself if your immediate thoughts and feelings align with those values. Finally, consider whether your original interpretation of the situation offers you the opportunity to act in some meaningful way. If it doesn't, revisit your alternative interpretations. Remember, the stories we tell ourselves shape our mental scripts and ultimately become our reality. So, if you tell yourself, "I'm the victim; things aren't fair; nothing ever goes right for me," chances are you'll find it near impossible to change your circumstances. Instead, think about what every situation can teach you (about yourself or life in general) and allow those new interpretations to empower you to act.

Reframing *my* thoughts

Remember, I'm sharing these strategies with you because I have had to overcome them in my own life, and they have helped me work through difficult times when my limited mindset prevented me from acting in my own best interest. I already had a master's in accounting, but I didn't want to live the rest of my life as a CPA, so I decided to go back to business school and get my MBA. I didn't want to go just anywhere, though. If I was going to do this, I was going to do it *right*, starting with applying to the best of the best business schools in the country.

I set my sights on a particularly prestigious school in the Northeast (you've probably heard of it), and I did everything in my power to get in. I talked with advisors, spoke with professors I knew who worked there, flew out to have lunch with some of my brothers' friends who had gone to that school, and even asked them for advice on how to rewrite my entry essay to give myself the best shot at getting accepted.

After all of that time and effort, I felt pretty good about my chances, which is why I was devastated when I got my rejection letter. I felt completely deflated, and I thought that I'd never be able to get into the world of private equity or consulting without a degree from a great school. As a victim of my limited mindset, I contemplated giving up on the pursuit of a new degree and doing something else entirely. My self-worth had taken a dive, but then I tried to look at things from a different perspective.

By *reframing* my thoughts, I began to realize that only a specific number of people get into that program, and perhaps there was someone else out there who needed to get into that program more than me, or there was another way I was supposed to learn those skills. Or maybe the reason I didn't get into the program was so I would have time to work on growing my consulting business or write another book (spoiler alert, I ended up doing both of those things!). Reframing my thoughts is what allowed me to let go of that idea and that specific goal so I could pursue other opportunities and achieve other great things. *And*, after I'd grown my business and written my second book, I still got into Duke University's MBA program, where I met some incredible people without whom I can't imagine my life.

When I thought I wasn't capable or good enough, I was afraid and felt powerless over my career choices, but when I realized that maybe I didn't need to get into that first school to be successful, my attitude changed, and that's why I was able to then behave in a way that ultimately helped me succeed.

How awesome would it be if we could break this toxic cycle? Well, we can, but it takes practice.

🧠 Exercise Your Knowledge

Think back to a time when you felt overwhelmed by stress. Let's say you were trying to make a deadline for a project, but you ran into an unexpected obstacle (hey, it happens!). Your first thought might be *I don't know how to fix this*. That's pretty tame, but maybe that thought causes you to feel a little apprehensive, which quickly spirals into *If I can't fix this, my boss will see how incompetent I am and fire me*. Well, darn. A minute ago, you just needed to find a solution, but now you're thinking you might need to find a new job.

When you find yourself in a downward spiral of negative thinking, you may be advised to try and control your thoughts. But it's impossible to control your thoughts, and it's exhausting to try. Even well-established mindfulness practices like meditation cannot stop negative thoughts from happening, so if you fixate on trying to stop unwanted thoughts from popping up, you'll end up in a losing game of bad thought Whac-A-Mole.

How can you use reframing in this situation to modify how your thoughts make you *feel*, even if you can't change the thoughts themselves?

Remember, how you feel is almost entirely determined by how you interpret your thoughts. So, that first thought of *I don't know how to fix this* could make you feel worried or anxious that you've suddenly got an additional thing to address. That anxiety then fuels another negative thought, which fuels another negative feeling, which ultimately leads you to behave in a counterproductive way. Perhaps you proceed without reframing your negative thoughts and it costs you an important promotion. If you don't practice trying to reframe your pattern of negative thinking, over time this creates a cycle of negative thoughts and feelings that fuels undesirable behaviors, which are much more difficult to modify.

CHAPTER 4

Obstacles to Your Path of Abundance

W ouldn't it be great if the path to abundance was an easy and straight route with no unpleasant encounters or setbacks? Heck yeah! Realistically, though, change isn't something that happens overnight. Change is a constant, gradual process that takes repetition, adaptation, and force. Think about how water erodes away entire mountains. Does it lap against the rock a few times and then say, "Humph, this is way too slow; I'm going to give up." No. Do weightlifters build muscle by doing a handful of reps and then calling it quits? No. These dramatic changes wouldn't be possible without consistency, motivation, or the ability to adapt to and overcome obstacles. We've already covered how reframing can help set you on the right path toward transforming your mindset from one of scarcity to one of abundance, but mental changes come with their own set of obstacles that you must overcome if you want to succeed.

> **Lightbulb Moment:** It may surprise you, but one of the biggest obstacles in your path to abundance can be your own ego. In psychoanalysis, the ego is the part of us that mediates between our desires and social expectations. It performs a difficult balancing act between how we perceive ourselves and how we want to be perceived by others. The irony is that our egos are incredibly vulnerable and susceptible to manipulation. When that happens, we often find ourselves behaving in a way that is not congruent with our true self, the self we want to be. Instead, we become greedy, jealous, and grandiose, fueled by the desire to become someone who is liked by others. And therein lies the problem. In an effort to satisfy our own self-esteem, we become someone else entirely. *Why?* It's because a corrupted ego is driven by the fear of not being, or not having, something.

Facing your ego

Marketing works by creating a false sense of anxiety in a potential customer that can only be relieved by purchasing the item being sold. Even if we're aware that that's how it works, we're still not immune to it. More than two-thirds of the US economy is driven by people buying things they don't need because as soon as there is something new to be wanted, they become fearful that they don't have it. It's a perfect system, and if it weren't so perfect, the entire economy would collapse. And here comes the rub: There will *always* be new things to buy. Our ego will always drive us toward immediate rewards and avoid delaying gratification at all costs. If we allow a corrupted ego to drive our actions, you can see how it could quickly destroy our relationship with money.

There is an old Chinese fable about a rice farmer who discovers a pair of golden chopsticks and takes them home with him. One day, while he's eating, he's admiring his chopsticks and suddenly feels insecure about the condition of his bowls and plates. He decides to replace them with the finest quality crockery he can find. The next day, while he's eating, he notices a few imperfections on his table and decides to replace that too. This pattern continues until the farmer has replaced every item of furniture in his house with newer, more lavish items, and his old house is completely and permanently gone. The moral of this story is that once we start down a path of material pursuit, we can never be truly satisfied. Our ego is only satisfied by the *next* thing we buy, and if we get into the trap of satisfying through spending, enough will never be enough. So, how do we overcome this obstacle and our propensity to spend? Simple. By changing our mindset. Well, it's simple but still not *easy*.

Giving up the pursuit of "things" allows us to also look inward and appreciate our ability to change and become something new, something different, something *better*—not through buying things but through *becoming* something. Material obsession teaches us to focus only on what we have, but what we truly desire is to be admired not for the things we have but for the quality of our being. Sure, I could define myself by my job title or by how many hours I work a week, and people may be impressed by that, but that stifles any opportunity to become something more than what I *do*. Who we actually are is the person we become when we strip away the material things we have and the boundaries of what we do.

Being fearful

Feeling satisfied with what we have rather than being fearful because of what we lack is a tricky place to get to, but if you can do this, it will change your life—*forever*. As far as emotions go, fear is unique in its ability to both motivate and paralyze us. What we fear, we fixate on, and what we fixate on, we manifest. Therefore, it is essential that we guard what we hold in our minds and what we bring into our reality. In all my years working with clients and their businesses, the most common fear people tell me they have is the fear of losing their money. They could have $15,000 in savings, or they could have $50,000,000 in savings. Whatever the amount is, it doesn't matter; we're all afraid of running out of money. In some ways, that fear keeps us motivated to keep working, keep earning, and keep saving, but in other ways, a fearful mindset can be disastrous when we focus on the worst possible outcome. But, as the following Check Yourself exercise illustrates, there is a way to overcome this fearful mindset—by using an outcome pyramid.

✓ CHECK YOURSELF

Let's return to the example of the job interview we used in chapter 3. There's no way to know for sure what the outcome of the interview will be, so you consider all the possibilities. Now, imagine the outcomes as a three-tiered pyramid. The widest level at the base is the most likely outcome, and the narrowest level at the top is the least likely. When you think catastrophically (i.e., with a fearful mindset), you trick yourself into believing that the worst possible outcome is the most likely. Realistically though, if you're confident in your abilities, behaviors, and actions, the most likely outcome is going to be the best one—the one that you've planned for and manifested. So, if you find yourself fixating on the worst possible outcome in a situation, picture this pyramid of outcomes in your mind and then flip it over. Now, the narrow point is on the bottom and the widest part is on the top. Using this mental exercise, you can talk yourself out of catastrophic thinking by reminding yourself that the worst possible outcome most likely has the smallest chance of happening.

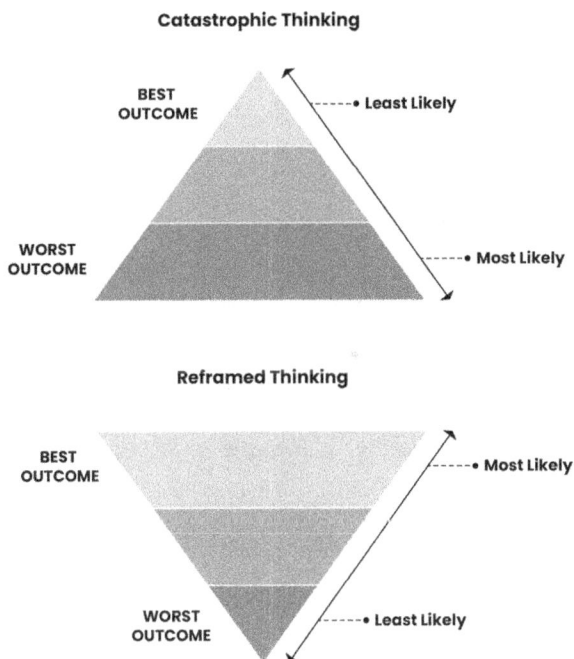

Catastrophic Thinking

BEST OUTCOME — Least Likely

WORST OUTCOME — Most Likely

Reframed Thinking

BEST OUTCOME — Most Likely

WORST OUTCOME — Least Likely

Figure 4.1. By flipping the outcome triangle upside down, you can reframe catastrophic thinking into a new set of beliefs full of faith, hope, and abundance.

The outcome pyramid shows us how we can flip our fears to avoid fixating on the worst possible outcome—which has an outsized influence on our imaginations but is usually the least likely to occur. The outcome pyramid doesn't just work in cases where the outcomes are static, though; it's a philosophy that can help you overcome fear as an obstacle in other areas of your life too. Every choice we make has an almost infinite number of possible outcomes.

Whether buying a house, starting a business, or expanding our network, if we focus on the worst possible outcome from the get-go, we will paralyze our opportunity for greatness. The next time you feel paralyzed by fear, imagine the worst possible outcome. Embrace that feeling, let go of resisting the fear, and come back to gratitude. Focus on your trajectory and on how the next thing you do will get you one step closer to abundance.

Lacking patience

We've now covered two major obstacles we can run into on the path to abundance and how to overcome them. Still, even if we learn how to deal with obstacles like ego and fear, there are other setbacks we must allow to just run their course. Patience, for example, is an obstacle many people overlook. They're so fixated on getting to the end goal that they rush the process. Truth be told, I'm probably one of the least patient people you'll ever come across. In fact, I often joke with my kids by saying, "I'll never be a doctor because I don't have any *patience*." I've always been good at figuring out what I want and how to get it and committed to working hard until I do. It's just that I like to go fast and achieve fast as well. You've probably heard of the Stanford marshmallow experiment on delayed gratification. Well, I can relate to those toddlers who cover their eyes until it's time to eat the marshmallow, because let's face it, it's incredibly frustrating to know what you want and how to get it, but be unable to. Patience is an obstacle we can't *act* on. We have no choice but to endure it. It's hard, though, because the longer we have to be patient, the less time we feel we have left.

Perhaps it's difficult to choose what to do with all the free time that comes with retirement, but the mindset of "it's too late to start" is one I forcefully disagree with. I know a founder of a real estate investment company who had his big break at sixty years old. Over a few years, he grew his company into a multibillion-dollar business. What if he'd given up at thirty? It is possible to find success (whatever that looks like for you) later in life. Sometimes, walking a different path for a while, such as taking a different job, brings us to the very crossroads we need to be successful. On the flip side, I meet with dozens of young people just starting out who are overtly battling with their patience. They'll say, "Steve, I'm already twenty-five and not successful yet. My startup is a complete failure. I'm never going to make it!" They're already in the mindset of "it's too late to make it big," and that mindset is what turns a lack of patience into an obstacle.

One obstacle we *can* control is what we sacrifice to stay true to our trajectory. Similar to giving up the pursuit of material items, we may have to sacrifice parts of our daily patterns to align our actions with our intentions. They don't have to be permanent sacrifices, but small, short-term changes can have a significant impact on how things turn out in the long run. Let me give you an example. In 2008, I was twenty-nine years old, working full-time on growing my business, and I decided it was time to go back to school and get my undergrad degree. I was determined to do it without going into debt, and I knew I'd have to make a few financial sacrifices for that to happen. At the time, the Taco Bell in the university's food court had a deal where I could buy two chicken burritos for $2.16 (with tax), and so, to save on money, I ate those two burritos *every single day* I was on campus. While other students were spending fifteen dollars on a fancy deli sandwich with all the fixings, plus a drink, chips, and a cookie, I was eating ninety-nine-cent burritos. Don't get me wrong, I could more than afford the fancy lunch, but I was committed to not overspending when I didn't have to. A few years later, when I went back and got my master's degree, I did the same thing, only this time with a little more culinary finesse. You may have heard of a PB&J, but have you ever heard of a P&PB&J? It's like a regular PB&J but with a handful of pretzels smushed between the bread.

Those were the sacrifices, or rather "snackrifices," I made to make sure I was spending as little extra money as possible. Now, I'm not saying you have to do exactly what I did (although you should try a P&PB&J sandwich at least *once* in your life), but what I'm trying to demonstrate is that patterns and mindset go together. It wasn't about the twelve dollars I saved by eating cheap food; it was that I was committed to a pattern that honored my mindset of "I'm not going to get into debt." At the end of the day, I didn't even need to dip into my savings to pay for school. Somehow, things worked out. New contracts or high-paying projects would come in, and I would jump on every opportunity that presented itself to me, even working eighteen-hour days for a few weeks here and there. I'd created my mindset, and that's why I was able to stick to the patterns that would get me what I wanted, even if that meant sacrificing things in the short term.

You don't have to sacrifice everything, though, and you don't even have to be sacrificing money. You may sacrifice your time on superfluous things to make time for the stuff that really matters— the *big* stuff. It's a balancing act between deciding what you're able to sacrifice in the here and now for things you want later on. Often, the little things we spend time, money, or resources on now are small in comparison to what we really want: a big dream, a big purchase, a big opportunity! Just like in the marshmallow experiment, delayed gratification is a muscle we can strengthen over time by making small, consistent sacrifices that bring us closer to what we actually want. If we're unable to do that, we're left stuck in a loop of instant gratification, which only satisfies our ego temporarily. At its core, sacrificing means focusing less on what you want to *have* or *do* and more on your *potential* to become something bigger and better.

I know people who, at sixty-five years old, are steadfast in the belief that they have no time left to achieve their goals. They've worked their entire life at a nine-to-five job, and now they feel like their life is over because they don't have anything left to *do*. My advice? Do everything! Granted, some things get more difficult to do as we get older, but realistically, after sixty-five, the average person still has fifteen years to do everything they want to do. That's still a sufficient amount of time! Write that book, walk (or run) a marathon, visit those friends, play with your children and grandchildren, travel to that country—and to that other one. Time will run out for all of us someday; that's a guarantee. Our time here on earth may not be infinite, but the list of things we can do with it that will bring us happiness is.

🧠 Exercise Your Knowledge

Take a moment to reflect on the sacrifices you've made in your life to be where you are right now. What sacrifices have you already made to get here? Are there any sacrifices you might still need to make to achieve the life you've always wanted? Write a list of sacrifices you've made and another list of potential sacrifices. Writing things down is a helpful tool to give yourself clarity on your goals and priorities, and it can also help you reassess what you want and how to get there. It's important to have intentions, but without knowing *how* to get them, chances are you may end up falling short of those goals.

CHAPTER 5

Letting Go to Get What You Want

You might be thinking, "Okay, Steve, now I've read about knowing what I want, the mindset I need to get there, how to overcome obstacles in my path, and knowing when to sacrifice things, but how can I turn mindset and patterns into concrete results? I understand why I shouldn't define myself by what I *have* and what I *do*, and I'm committed to a desire to become *something more*. So, how do I get what I want?"

> **Lightbulb Moment:** We will encounter many obstacles on the path to what we desire, but none so big as the desire itself. When we focus our energy on the *wanting* we have for something, our desire becomes the thing that blocks our path to obtaining it. The only way to overcome that obstacle and clear the path ahead of us is to grab on tightly to the desire, feel the weight of it, recognize the way it consumes us, and then . . . *let it go.*

Power of letting go

As part of a master class she gave in 2011, Oprah Winfrey related the incredibly moving story about how her desire to join the cast of the movie *The Color Purple* almost completely derailed her sense of self.[1] She was taken by the book the minute she read it and became overwhelmed by the prospect of trying to get involved in the production of the movie adaptation. At the time she wasn't the prominent celebrity she is today, but she was dead set on wanting to be involved in the movie someway, somehow. She went on to talk about how she prayed every day to God for an opportunity to turn her desire into a reality. To her delight, after months of praying, she was picked up by one of the casting directors and asked to audition for a lead part in the movie. All of her prayers were being answered, tenfold. She was certain this was her sign from God. But then, months went by without a follow-up word about her audition or the movie. She became completely consumed with her desire to get the part. Day and night, she thought about it, praying for an answer or another sign. When the waiting became too much, she hastily called up the casting director, who told her in no uncertain terms that he had "real actresses" to audition for the part. This rejection only made her want the part even more.

She told herself that if she was thinner, they'd reconsider her for the role, so she made plans to join a weight-loss program where she spent two full weeks pushing herself to become *someone else*. By that time, she was all but convinced the part was going to go to someone else, but her desire still burned. Then one day, as she was running, she began to pray again.

"Please God," she said, "Help me let this go." And with every step she took, she said to herself, "I need to let this go. I need to let this go. Help me let this go." The skies opened and rain began to fall, but she carried on, still praying as she ran. She repeated her prayer until she'd run two more miles and could neither run nor pray anymore.

"I surrender it all to you, my savior," she said, finally giving up the desire she had been clinging to for months. Perhaps it was divine intervention or fate, but whatever you choose to call it, the moment she surrendered everything up to a power that was bigger than her, everything changed. Her path became clearer. Inside the wellness center, a phone rang, and on the other end was the director, Steven Spielberg himself, calling to offer her the part.

Just like with our ego, when we desire something, we're subconsciously telling ourselves that we don't have it, that we *lack* it. Unless we can let go of the feeling of wanting, we won't be able to open ourselves up to receiving whatever it is we desire. This is because our minds will be focused on what we lack, our fears, and our limitations instead of the opportunities that are right before us. How do we know if our desire for something is becoming an obstacle to achieving it? Instead of focusing on how badly we want something, we can set the intention to have something, admit to ourselves that we desire it, believe that we will receive it, and then turn it over to a *higher power*. It can be God, the Universe, alien fungi, but whatever it is, we have to take the *wanting* and put it somewhere out of our control, because it's impossible to make any progress if we're trying to control our desire. In fact, if we try too hard, that desire will eventually control us. Life is full of these little contradictions, and the truth is, we get what we want when we stop insisting on it.

Remember that just being alive is a miraculous thing, and existing on this planet exactly when and as who we are is in and of itself something to marvel at. There are an infinite number of paths we can choose in life that will lead us to any destination we set our minds to. When we make peace with being okay with whether something happens or doesn't, we clear the path ahead of us and can walk freely. That's not to say the obstacles we encounter will always be in our control, but in surrendering our desires, we get rid of all the negativity and fear associated with not having those desires, and we remind ourselves that we are infinite beings, not subject to trying to control the obstacles in our path. We can overcome them *without* controlling them. Sure, terrible things can and do happen— recessions, unemployment, divorce, and so on—but when we stop trying to force things to turn out a certain way, we can accept them for what they are. And that's where the biggest changes happen.

✓ CHECK YOURSELF

Picture your dream house, the bigger, the better. Get creative as you imagine how it looks without limits, obstacles, or restrictions. Be as specific as possible with the details. How many bedrooms are there? Is there a pool, a tennis court, a bowling alley? What do the finishes look like? What type of floors are there? Visualize everything. Now, instead of focusing on how much you desire that house (or how much you don't have it), let that house go. Tell yourself how hard you're going to work to get that house—and then let it go. Set the intention to get the house and know that if you don't get that house, there will be something better waiting for you.

Turning pain into purpose

Letting go of what you want or relinquishing control over your desire isn't always easy. There will be times in your life when you set the intention to have something, turn the desire over to a higher power, work like crazy for what you want, and then still end up not getting to where you want to be. It can feel like you've been in a boxing ring with every possible obstacle and made it nine rounds only to lose the fight right at the end. Losing is painful, not just because our egos hate it, but physiologically too. Our brains are literally wired to feel loss more intensely than victory, and if we can hack into that pain, we can use it as motivation to act. Turning pain into purpose is a crucial skill to have because if we don't learn how to take painful situations and turn them into something meaningful, our progress stops with the pain.

In 2021, I went through one of the most difficult, painful experiences of my life. The details are irrelevant, and I'm being intentionally vague because I want to focus on the process that I used to let it go, but it was a total blindside that completely destroyed my sense of self-worth. I'd been through some difficult times, but trying to find a way to deal with the trauma of what had happened almost broke me. I was hurting, and that pain controlled me. It made it impossible to trust other people, be confident in who I was, or communicate with friends, family, and clients (which made doing business very difficult). I replayed the moment over and over in my head like a private screening of the worst movie in the world. I would go to bed thinking about it, and when I woke up, it only took a few moments for it to creep back into my headspace.

It consumed my every waking moment, too, making me physically sick on more than one occasion. It was the most vulnerable I've ever felt, but it was more than that. I couldn't get away from my feelings, and so, over time the darkness I felt began to envelop me like a big blanket of sadness. The person who had hurt me was long gone, and yet here I was letting them still control my thoughts and feelings. I needed to let this thing go. In case you're wondering, I did go to therapy to help me cope with the trauma, including EMDR (eye movement desensitization and reprocessing), a fascinating technique used to literally recode distressing memories and store them safely with other long-term memories instead of in the brain's "fear center." I also found some helpful tools through hypnotherapy. However, despite this professional help, the pain and hurt persisted.

A lot of research talks about the benefits of nature for our well-being, so in the past, I've done what I call "think weeks," when I unplug from all the corporate noise and go someplace really isolated and peaceful to reset my mind and body. I had limited time at this point in my life, so I found myself a beautiful spot in my home state of Colorado for a "think day." In a secluded spot shaded by the canopy of a giant fir tree in front of a river, I was totally alone—just me, my thoughts, and my oversized emotional baggage. I got out my journal and for the next few hours wrote down every single thought and feeling that had been consuming me up to that point. I knew that if I didn't find a way to let this go, I was going to self-destruct . . . literally.

I'm a huge advocate for journaling and meditation when try-ing to clear a cloudy head. Writing everything down somehow takes abstract thoughts and turns them into physical things that are now separated from us. I spent some time thinking about what it was that was making it so difficult to let go. I had every intention and desire to, but something was blocking my path. I thought that if I let it go, then the perpetrator was winning and I was saying I was okay with the fact that they hurt me. As I meditated on this thought, I realized that the memories I was holding on to were what was poisoning me and making me feel so awful. The betrayal had come and gone, but I had let the pain linger inside me for months and months until I didn't even know where traumatized Steve ended and normal, happy Steve began. Sitting at that river with my thoughts and feelings now tangible in my journal, I made a conscious decision to let it all go. "I'm not going to hold on to this anymore," I said aloud. "I am let-ting this go, today." And then I imagined taking all that negativity I was holding on to and throwing it into the river in front of me. I sat for another moment, watching the water carry my pain downstream and out of sight. I had let it go. I was free.

I didn't just forget about the trauma, though. It's impossible to stop thoughts, remember? Sometimes I catch myself noticing a memory from that experience creeping into my head. The difference is that now the feelings I associate with that trauma are powerless. I was able to reframe those thoughts by changing the feelings and the meaning I associated with them, and in doing that, I was able to let them go. Let me be clear: It's okay to feel hurt, pain, and other negative emotions associated with the things that happen to us. It's also okay to take the time to heal. It's not like I experienced this trauma and was able to let it go the next day; it took time. I just wish I would have let it go sooner so I didn't waste precious time stuck in the past. Similar to the way letting go of desire clears the path ahead of us, letting go of pain creates room for us to be still and makes a place for us to receive all the world has to offer.

Exercise Your Knowledge

The world is an incredibly noisy place that will overwhelm us if we let it. We can fill up our day with our jobs, the news, relationships, hobbies, and social media, but it's crucial to give yourself a few moments each day to be still. It doesn't matter whether you're the richest person in the world or the poorest, being still will allow you to reflect on where you are on your path now and express gratitude for it. Unexpected moments out of our control can leave us feeling fearful or hurt, and if we get consumed by those experiences, we shut out the world and all the abundant things it has to offer us.

Take a moment to practice being still. Not just physically but mentally too. Sit wherever you're most

continued

comfortable—maybe it's in your favorite chair or on a windowsill where you can see out into your neighborhood. Clear your mind and just breathe, in and out. Don't fixate on what just happened or on the next thing you must do. Just be present, focused on the here and now. Let go of the things you've been holding on to. Acknowledge any thoughts that pop into your mind and then return to a clear mental space. Be still.

PART II

Becoming Financially Fit

Six Drivers of Financial Fitness

F inancial fitness goes beyond just having enough money to buy whatever you want, whenever you want. It means having the knowledge and the skills to manage your finances in a way that your immediate and long-term goals are met. We've covered how important an abundant mindset is and how to overcome obstacles in our path to abundance, but having a solid strategy is pivotal to becoming someone who is financially fit.

While there's no single, identical strategy to follow to achieve financial success, I guarantee that each strategy will include the same key components and cover the same key steps—the six drivers of financial fitness. Regardless of where you started, where you are now, or where you're aiming to be financially, you can use the six drivers of financial fitness to develop a solid financial strategy. By following this financial fitness model (illustrated on the next page), you will gain a better understanding of what to plan for, where to invest, and how to minimize future financial burdens on yourself.

Here's a brief description of the six drivers of financial success and what each part entails:

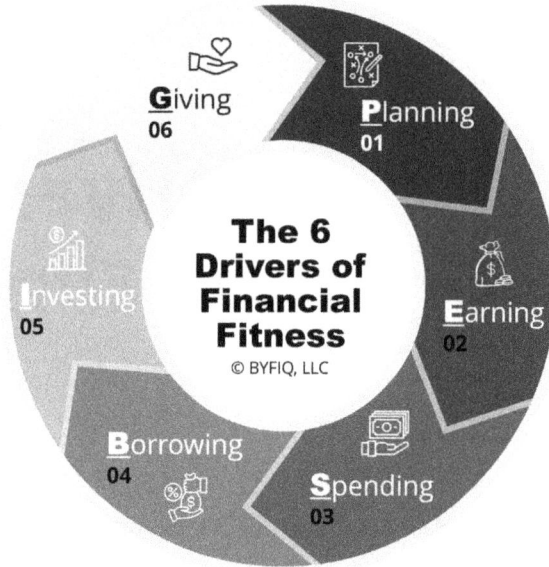

Figure 6.1. The financial fitness model empowers individuals to lead better lives by improving their planning, earning, spending, borrowing, investing, and giving habits, thus fostering a healthier and more secure financial future.

Planning: This involves creating a go-forward plan for your life, including items such as your musts and beliefs, unique ability, strategic problem, strategy, and goals, as well as developing a budget or financial forecast that will support your plan.

Earning: This means maximizing your earning potential to ensure you have the means not just to survive but to *thrive*.

Spending: This includes learning how to spend according to your values rather than your ego and being mindful that you don't "out-lifestyle" your income.

Borrowing: This means recognizing the dangers of things like digital money, learning how to avoid the "interest sinkhole," and using leverage to maximize your returns.

Investing: This includes being aware of how investing can help (or hinder) you on your journey to abundance.

Giving: This means celebrating your ability to give money, time, and talent to meaningful causes while also caring for yourself and those who mean the most to you.

Over the next six chapters, we'll discuss the importance of each of these components and how they help shape your financial fitness.

CHAPTER 7

Planning

Whenever I hear people say, "I can't change the future," I can't help but think, *Well, of course you can; that's what planning is.* Planning for your future doesn't mean having every moment of your life mapped out in front of you, but it does give you the ability to set large goals and break them down into smaller, incremental decisions that will help get you from where you are to where you want to be. Having a plan isn't just about setting goals for yourself, though, because how you arrive at what those goals are requires a certain amount of planning too. That's why, for years, I've relied on a "go-forward plan" to help define my direction, set my intentions, and ultimately guide which specific goals I choose to set.

> **Lightbulb Moment:** In a nutshell, a go-forward plan puts into perspective what you want to achieve (in life or in business) and how you plan on bringing those goals to fruition. While being ambitious and setting goals is a crucial part

continued

of creating the life you want, the go-forward plan is really about creating a strategic life plan to literally go forward toward your potential and a life of abundance.

Defining your musts

Creating a go-forward plan starts with defining your musts and beliefs. If you aren't sure what that means, you might find it worthwhile to do a little soul-searching first. Spend some time asking yourself the "big" questions, and answer them as honestly as you can: Who am I? What do I treasure most? What are the personal principles I must honor to stay true to who I am? Some answers may come easily, and others might surprise you (that's okay!), but a little introspection goes a long way when it comes to creating a go-forward plan that is meaningful and specific to *you*. The reason I start with identifying your individual musts is because they are the foundation of nonnegotiable rules that inform how you approach your life.

Your unique list of musts does two important things: First, it can be used as an internal moral compass, helping guide every decision you make, from the opportunities you vehemently chase after to the ones you say no to. Second, and perhaps more importantly, your musts act as an informal measuring stick to help you gauge to what extent you are living the life you truly want. Crucially, and I can't stress this enough, musts are not the *things* we desire. A giant house, a fancy car, and other material luxuries aren't (or shouldn't be) imperative to you living your most fulfilling life. Rather, your musts are a collection of self-set principles that reflect your personal beliefs and encourage you to pursue choices that honor your values.

Some of my personal musts include continuously seeking growth and personal improvement, taking care of my physical and mental health, and acting with kindness. Since these examples reflect a few of my core values, such as family, vitality, and personal growth, these musts set the tone for how I live my life. They are the things that, above everything else, I will not compromise on. Musts are a little different than values, though, and that's because, depending on the situation, values can be *flexible*. For example, you might value integrity but be too uncomfortable to tell your boss that you're unhappy at work. Musts, on the other hand, have to remain steadfast. Hopefully that makes the distinction clear.

Why is it important to have a clear understanding of your musts? Well, they allow you to identify when you aren't honoring your true self. When you behave contrary to your musts, you typically feel uncomfortable and even discontent with your life. For me, if I'm not growing or learning or improving myself in some way, I start feeling out of sorts very quickly because I know I'm not aligning my behavior with my musts. Instead, I'm acting contrary to them. As a consequence, I get depressed, find it difficult to stay motivated, and struggle to keep my sights fixed on my life's higher purpose. I'm passionate about taking care of my health because I want to be able to play with my grandchildren when that time comes, and showing up for others with empathy and gentleness is the key to making authentic connections with people I cross paths with, so when I'm not acting in accordance with these musts, I feel very detached from myself and the people around me.

The reason we get uncomfortable when we don't honor our musts is that it is impossible to hold two opposing beliefs in our mind at once. We just can't do it. For instance, if you tell people you're an ambitious person, but you're stuck in a job you hate because it stifles your ability to pursue what you really want, guess what? You're going to wind up feeling unhappy because your expectations don't align with your reality. If that still feels a little confusing, remember that on the surface, your musts are the more tangible, concrete things you can feel, see, and experience, but underneath, these musts reflect your deeper values and that's why you cannot waver on them. Instead, you can use your musts as a sort of litmus test to assess whether or not you're doing what's right for you. And anytime there's a conflict between who you are and who you *believe* you are, there's going to be discontent. That uncomfortable feeling is like a little warning light that comes on when it's time to realign yourself with your musts.

I was high above the Atlantic Ocean, flying home from a trip to Europe, when all of a sudden, my own warning light came on. It was a few days after my fortieth birthday, and I'd just published my second book. At the time, I was the CFO of a billion-dollar construction and renewable energy company in Chattanooga, Tennessee. Objectively, things were going great for me, *really* great, but crammed into a tiny airplane seat 35,000 feet above the ground, I began to feel very ill at ease. Completely disconnected from any distractions from work or my phone, for the next eight hours I was a hostage to my own thoughts. *What am I doing with my life?* The question seemed to come out of nowhere. I was personally and professionally on top of my game, but something inside me just didn't feel quite right.

As I reflected on this feeling, I realized that, despite being proud of what I had accomplished, I felt disconnected from something that mattered more than anything to me: my family. Back in Colorado, my mom and five of my six siblings and all their kids were living a life I felt totally separate from. It bothered me that my kids had cousins they didn't really know, and it really bothered me that I was living a life that didn't honor my musts. Granted, the paycheck was great, but all the money in the world wasn't worth passing up opportunities to grow, pursue improvement, and be close to the people I love. Those were my *musts*, and it was time to realign my life with them. I was two months shy of my next big bonus, but I made the decision to walk away in order to stay true to who I was. Within four months, I'd given thirty days' notice at my job, sold my house, packed up everything, and moved my wife and kids back to Colorado. The moral of this story is that opportunities will arise, people will come into your life, job offers and business partnerships will come and go, but unless you have your musts properly defined, you may not be able to recognize whether or not a decision is right for you.

Discovering your purpose

Once you've identified your nonnegotiable musts, and you're confident in what you need to do in order to be true to yourself, the next step in the go-forward plan is to work through your limiting beliefs. These might include thinking you're not smart enough, good enough, or valuable enough to go after what you want. When I left my CFO job in Chattanooga, I had plenty of my own limiting beliefs: a tiny voice in the back of my mind telling me I was irresponsible for turning down a bunch of money, reckless for moving my family across the country (again), and not clever enough to succeed on my own, even though I'd done exactly that many times before. The truth is, limiting beliefs arise from fear-driven scarcity mindsets. And if you listen to those beliefs, they will lead you down a path of compromising on your musts and ultimately sabotaging your happiness. Learning to overcome our inclination to self-sabotage goes back to harnessing the power of reframing and using those techniques to change how we think, feel, and behave. Knowing how to reframe limiting beliefs is essential to planning, because when you hold on to limiting ideas and fears, what you're really doing is holding yourself back from achieving what you already know you deserve. Once you clear your mind of all the possible things that might go wrong, you'll be better equipped to reflect on what your unique abilities are and how they can uncover your purpose.

A unique ability is a special talent, capability, or characteristic that makes you different from others and enables you to fulfill your own purpose. I believe that everyone on earth has their own unique talent. Whether it's the ability to make art, tell a great story, or take conceptual problems and come up with tangible solutions, an abundance of unique talents lives inside each of us, just waiting to be uncovered and turned into a *purpose*. Some people uncover their talents and realize their purpose early on in life, but most people (maybe even you) don't know what their purpose is, and that's because they aren't entirely sure what their unique abilities are. If you're hoping for a step-by-step guide on how to uncover your unique abilities, then you're in luck! Just complete the steps in the following "Exercise Your Knowledge" box.

Exercise Your Knowledge

Figuring out what your unique abilities are starts with doing a little research. This list isn't exhaustive, but it's a great starting point:

1. Make a list of people you are close to. It can be family, friends, colleagues . . . whoever you think *knows* you best.

2. Send a message to each of them asking what *they* think your unique abilities are.

3. Spend time answering the question on your own. This might involve doing a little self-discovery, journaling,

or taking a personality test like the Myers-Briggs Type Indicator.

4. When you have all the responses, compile and organize the answers, paying close attention to where responses overlap and then try to identify what the underlying themes are. For example, when I did this exercise for myself, I came up with these four unique abilities:

   a. Positive, empathetic light of influence

   b. Ambitious learner, grounded in generosity and compassion

   c. Big-picture thinker with a fierce resolve to act

   d. Highly organized "numbers guy" capable of communicating with precision

Remember though, the point of this exercise isn't to come up with as many unique abilities as you can. Instead, it's about giving yourself the time to reflect and the space to understand and appreciate your uniqueness.

Chances are you'll discover you have more than one unique ability, and from there, you can identify what's unique about you and what your strengths are. Then, when you use these strengths to go out into the world and *act on* your unique abilities, *that's* when you'll discover your purpose.

Identifying obstacles

By gaining a better sense of your purpose, you can take the next step in the go-forward plan: identifying the underlying issue that stands in your way of fulfilling that purpose and achieving your most important goals. For example, perhaps you feel like you're battling several smaller problems related to your finances; maybe you're struggling to pay your bills or keep your credit card balance down. While these are definitely obstacles in your path to a financially successful future, the overarching issue is that you likely aren't making enough money every month to cover these expenses. Now, it's important to remember that overarching problems are different from limiting beliefs—they can be systemic or circumstantial obstacles and overcoming them requires resources beyond cognitive reframing. The reason it's so important to be aware of the "bigger problem" is that if you aren't able to resolve the more pressing issue, you will continue to face smaller, related obstacles that will ultimately prevent you from becoming your most successful, happy, and fulfilled self.

Overcoming your most significant problem starts with trying to identify the *overarching* issue that may be contributing to what you're struggling with. And the truth is, when you home in on what the bigger problem is, chances are you'll realize that it's something you can overcome with a bit of strategy and effort. For example, you may realize that your income is limited because you lack the education, skills, or financial resources you need to secure a job that allows you to financially support your family. Or perhaps the obstacles you're facing are a product of your surroundings. You may live in a town that is far away from opportunities for you to pursue a career in your field, or you might have a job you like but work in a hostile environment that leaves you feeling drained and unfulfilled. Obstacles come in many shapes and forms, but once you've defined your overarching issue, the next step is to identify what you must do to defend against the obstacle and determine what the consequences will be if you don't succeed. It may seem counterproductive to focus on potential consequences, but if you don't outline them, it will be hard for you to stay accountable to your plan. Here are two scenarios of how to identify an overarching problem and map out a potential solution:

Financial scenario: It's becoming increasingly difficult to pay my bills every month. If I don't find a way to earn more money, I'm going to wind up deeper in debt, which will damage my financial future.

Personal scenario: My obligations at work are interfering with my ability to spend time with my loved ones. If I don't get help or learn to delegate some of these tasks, I will burn out and damage my most important relationships.

Learning how to properly identify and define your problem is a crucial part of your planning phase, because if you don't emphasize the consequences of *not* overcoming your problem, you may never find the motivation to do so. Education is a very common obstacle, which is why it might surprise you that planning for your education doesn't have to mean going to college. If you're unsure if college is right for you, start with taking some courses and give yourself the time to explore what type of subjects or material you gravitate toward. Do you love economics? Computers? Are you doing better in a life-science subject?

Maybe the answer is none of the above. Remember, learning a trade is a perfectly legitimate vocation, and a lot of people make a six-figure income doing just that. I learned a trade of my own over one summer in high school. While all my friends were enjoying their vacations, going to the beach, and hanging out, I was installing sprinkler systems. I learned so much on the job that I actually started my own business the following summer: Steve's Sprinklers. (We'll circle back to that later on.) For now, let's say you want to become a doctor or a lawyer; something like that requires a very specific plan. Bottom line: Don't let school interfere with your education. Roughly one in four Americans (23.5 percent) have a bachelor's degree as their highest level of education, and the percentage with a doctorate is around half that (13.1 percent).[1] That means that a majority of people in the United States have landed their career *without* a fancy degree.

The good news is that understanding what your main problem is, and knowing what is keeping you from reaching your true potential, will help you identify a meaningful and effective solution to the problem. On the other hand, the bad news (or rather, the "fine print") is that once you resolve that one big problem—say you get a higher-paying job and you're able to pay off your credit cards and have a little more financial freedom—there will always be another problem down the road that you'll have to overcome too. And that's okay! Because learning how to identify an overarching strategic problem is the first step in formulating thoughtful, intentional goals that will help you overcome those obstacles.

Determining a life strategy

Once you've defined your primary obstacles, the next step in the go-forward plan is establishing a life strategy. This is where you start to put all the components together—your musts, your purpose, and your overarching problem to overcome. What does a good life strategy look like? At its core, a good life strategy is comprehensive, resilient, and flexible. It should be something that will guide you as you set specific goals but will also allow you to pivot and progress when you need to. There are four main components of developing a good strategy, starting with establishing a shared vision. In business, when you talk about having a "shared vision," it means you are taking into account *everyone* at the company—not just yourself or the executives or the stakeholders. You must consider everyone, especially your customers. Similarly, in life, when creating a shared vision, you must be mindful of and take into account who your personal stakeholders are. Maybe it's your spouse or your kids or your parents. These are the people you need to look out for and make sure you're considering in your shared vision.

What does winning look like? Not just for you, but for *everyone*? Just like in business, you have stakeholders in your own life who will be affected by your go-forward plan, so creating a winning strategy that works for everyone is paramount. If you don't, chances are you might still end up achieving your goals, but it might mean jeopardizing your values or falling short of your musts. For some people, winning might mean retiring at forty, or having half a dozen children, or opening a yoga studio. Winning is entirely subjective—it will look different for me and different for you, but identifying what your personal shared version of winning looks like will inform the rest of your strategy.

Once you've defined your vision, the second component in a good strategy is to consider where you're at in life relative to that vision. Remember that gratitude is an essential part of having an abundant mindset, so it's important to reflect on your place in life without any judgment. Think about what your life looks like from an intellectual, physical, social, financial, and spiritual perspective and be aware of how these complement or complicate your vision. Is being physically fit important to your vision? Is it necessary for you to have a strong social circle or feel spiritually connected to a higher power? Consider whether you currently have the intellectual and fiscal capabilities to achieve that vision now and if you don't, think about how you might tailor your strategy to secure them.

If that seems obvious, here's the part most people overlook when it comes to developing an effective strategy: being specific. It may sound similar to what I said about having to define your overarching problem to identify what your goals are, but it bears repeating here: If you don't get specific about defining what is standing in the way of your vision, then it will continue to be a vague, abstract obstacle that keeps you from fulfilling it. When you're able to pinpoint exactly what it is you need (or need to do) in order to pursue that vision, that's when you'll empower yourself to act.

The third part of a good strategy is to evaluate your current behaviors to determine what you should start, stop, and continue doing to make sure you're staying on a path to success (whatever that looks like to you). The patterns of our daily life will ultimately determine whether we exceed our vision or fall short. Do your daily patterns match your ultimate goals? If they don't, perhaps it's time to get real with yourself about how you can adjust your current behaviors so they serve your vision. These don't have to be patterns relating to a job or money. If winning to you means being able to eat dinner every night around a table with your loved ones, that's a perfectly legitimate behavior to prioritize.

Finally, the last step of creating a good strategy is to identify the specific resources, capabilities, and skill sets you need to be successful. It can mean anything from going back to school and getting a second degree to taking a course on customer communication or whatever skills are relevant to the career and lifestyle you want. My advice? Never settle. Regardless of what career you're pursuing, always set the intention of becoming the best version of yourself. Otherwise, why start? After playing his last game, Michael Jordan, one of the best basketball players of all time, was asked, "What sets you apart, Michael . . . Is it your God-given talent, ability, skill? What is it?" Jordan responded simply, "I have a lot of talent, a lot of God-given talent, a lot of skill. I worked really hard. But really, it's my standards. Every day, I demand more from myself than anybody else could humanly expect. I'm not competing with somebody else. I'm competing with what I'm capable of."[2]

The same advice can be applied to each of us as well. You don't want to be an average business professional, plumber, nurse, teacher, massage therapist, investment banker (or whatever); you want to be the best version you can be. And to be clear, being "the best" *doesn't* mean spending ridiculous amounts of money on superficial things in an effort to try and keep up with or compete with others. Not only would doing something like that be financially irresponsible, it's also not the smartest move from a business perspective because of something called *competitive convergence*. In business, competing companies within a particular industry often start adopting new strategies or changing their products or business models over time in an effort to "be the best." Then, to try and keep up with the new standards, other companies start making similar changes, and as a result, the differences between competitors decrease and businesses become even *more* similar (in terms of their pricing and other product or service offerings). And that's where a lot of businesses go wrong because in an effort to keep up with trying to be the best, companies miss out on opportunities to differentiate themselves and focus on other, more important areas, such as being innovative.

So, the take-home message here is that if it's a choice between being "the best" and being different, you'll be more successful if you focus on finding ways that make you stand out rather than trying to keep up with competing businesses. Part of that might mean evolving your skills to meet the demands on people in your field—not just right now but five or ten years down the line. Stay in tune with the trajectory of your field so you don't one day wake up and realize you're no longer on the right path to get what you want. Are there skills you can invest your time and resources into learning so you have the upper hand for what's next? At the same time, think about the lifestyle you want and whether that complements or complicates your career plans. Does your plan to work eighty hours a week align with your desire to start a family? How much freedom will traveling for work give you to spend time with your loved ones or take care of your health? By visualizing the lifestyle you want, you can get a better understanding of how to plan for the career and education you need to get there.

✓ **CHECK YOURSELF**

What are your musts? What is unique about you? What is the overarching problem you're facing and how are you going to overcome it? Knowing the answers to these questions is vital to putting your go-forward plan into action. It may take some time to figure them out, and that's okay, but these answers are fundamental to creating a strategy for your life. It's important to recognize that creating a life strategy isn't about trying to predict your future; it's about preparing yourself to be able to pursue intentional goals and embrace emerging opportunities simultaneously. So many incredible things have happened in my life that were never on my goal list, and I was able to say yes to them because I knew that 1) they aligned with my musts, and 2) my strategy allowed me the flexibility to take on unexpected opportunities.

Setting your goals

It should be pretty clear by now that a lot more goes into planning than meets the eye, and that's why I think a lot of people struggle to strategize successfully. It doesn't matter what your end goal looks like; getting there has to start with knowing these four things: what you want, where you're at now, the patterns you need to follow to be successful, and the resources you need to achieve your vision. Once you've got these four components figured out, then and only then are you ready to set some goals.

Most people want to rush into setting goals before they even know what their specific vision is, but the truth of the matter is that goals are really the last and final step to creating a go-forward plan. Once you've figured out your personal strategy, setting goals will ensure that your energy and ambition are focused on achieving something specific. As you continue to feel the satisfaction of achieving those specific goals, that motivation will become the momentum you need to continue moving toward that long-term vision. Certainly, setting SMART goals (specific, measurable, achievable, relevant, and time-sensitive) is necessary to gauge your progress and assess whether you need to adjust your strategy, but the big-picture thing I want you to realize is this: Your goals help you implement your strategy. Your strategy is there to help you overcome your overarching problem—the thing that gets in the way of your acting on your unique abilities or that violates your musts in some way. So, if you are determined to achieve your vision and have that big-picture life, you must start by looking inward to understand who you are, what you want, and what stands in your way—and expand from there.

Creating a budget

Now that you've identified your musts, your overarching problem, your strategy, and your goals, what's missing? In addition to your go-forward plan, you need to create a financial budget that is relevant and realistic and outlines how you're going to achieve those goals. What makes economic sense for one person won't necessarily help someone else, so tailoring your financial budget to your specific goals is essential. Let's assume, for example, that your go-forward plan is to help you earn more money so you can avoid getting into more debt. To do that, you decide you need to go back to school to earn another degree so you can secure a higher-paying job and earn more money. In addition to the cost of pursuing further education, you also need to account for where you'll stay and how much that will cost you, how you'll pay your bills in the meantime, whether you'll need to take on more debt, and how you're going to fulfill any other regular expenses.

It can be overwhelming to have to consider how you'll cover all these expenses without a concrete plan, but that's why creating a financial budget that complements your go-forward plan is so valuable. I know that the term *budget* has negative connotations because it's associated with ideas of scarcity and restrictiveness. That's why I prefer to use the term *financial forecast*. Instead of feeling rigid and stringent, this term encourages people to think about their future financial expectations and ambitions and then create a plan that's realistic *and* rooted in achieving those goals. Keep in mind, though, that determining what your earnings and expenses are going to be over the next twelve to twenty-four months will allow you to know how much money you're going to have or going to need to have in advance so you can plan accordingly. It's an easy step to overlook in planning, but keeping a financial forecast will give you the clarity to budget according to your means and be confident in your ability to meet your current and future financial obligations.

When setting a realistic financial budget, remember to keep your musts in mind. How and where you spend your money is up to you, but if you're going through the effort of figuring out what your musts are, developing a go-forward plan, and setting goals that honor those musts and you're not proactive about creating and sticking to a realistic budget or you're frequently overspending on superfluous things, then you're going to wind up living contrary to your musts, and it's going to be difficult to turn your vision into reality. So, plan according to your needs, but budget according to your means. I think instead of "I can't change the future," what people really mean is "I can't predict the future," and that's where they're right. Unfortunately, no amount of planning can help you prophesize what your education, career, or life will ultimately look like, but if you spend a little time planning and budgeting, you can get pretty darn close.

🧠 Exercise Your Knowledge

Creating a budget that is suitable for your personal financial forecast can be intimidating and overwhelming. Fortunately, I've outlined a few key steps to keep in mind that will help you stay on track:

1. Identify your goals. Reflect on your financial objectives, both short-term and long-term.

2. List your essentials. Write down must-have expenses for your basic needs.

3. Assess your discretionary spending. Take a look at what you're spending on nonessential expenses and allow that to guide where to cut back (if possible).

4. Create your budget. Allocate funds to your essentials first, then prioritize other financial goals.

5. Regularly review and adjust. This step is arguably the most important. Your financial situation will fluctuate from time to time, so tracking your progress and making changes as needed are essential.

6. Stay committed and flexible. This step serves to remind you to refer back to step 5 as needed. If you find yourself struggling to stick to your budget, or needing to adapt to unexpected situations, don't panic. Creating a realistic budget means recognizing that there will be expenses you don't plan for.

CHAPTER 8

Earning

When you read the word *earning*, you may assume it means what your annual salary is or how much money you can put into your bank account after taxes. When I read that word, though, I imagine that it includes all of the earning potential we hold within ourselves—and that's a much bigger number. As I'm writing this book, countries all over the world are on the brink of a recession. War, interest rate hikes, and large economic and financial disruptions like inflation have the majority of people waiting on the edge of their seats for what's to come. Warren Buffett famously said that during periods of inflation, the wisest decision we can make is to invest in ourselves and in our *earning power*. My goal is to show you how to extend this philosophy not just to periods of inflation, but to your entire life.

> **Lightbulb Moment:** The term *earning power* sounds complex and abstract, but in reality, it just refers to your unique skill set and how you can use it to maximize your *earning*

continued

potential (which includes things like your skills, training, and expertise) that, in turn, will maximize your earnings.

Increasing your earning potential

Looking back, I've always sought for ways to maximize my earning potential, even in seemingly innocuous situations. For example, every Saturday night, regardless of what else we had going on, my mom, my six siblings, and I would sit around our living room table for game night. When it was my night to choose, I'd always pick Monopoly, and I'd always make the game last as long as possible. What started out as an innocent board game would quickly become an elaborate web of side deals and under-the-table schemes that were against the rules. They weren't strictly against the rules of business, though, so I'd bend the rules to make sure I was always maximizing my earnings. I didn't just throw out the rule book; I changed the whole game. I would convince my siblings to sell properties to me by promising them five free turns to land on that square without paying rent, and if they weren't keen on that deal, I'd enter into partnerships with them. If they needed my purple card to buy a property, I'd give it to them on the condition that we be equal investors for any hotels that were built there and split any of the profits. These games would go on for *days*. I remember delicately sliding the board underneath my bed so we could keep the pieces in order and resume the next day. It seems wild, but I was really vehement about money management, making deals, and having the skills to make smart investments.

When I got to high school, it was no different. I would buy a six-pack of soda for a dollar and then sell them to kids on the school bus for a dollar apiece. It was a brilliant little scheme, and I made a few dollars doing that until the bus driver snitched on me, and I got into trouble for it. I didn't let that stop me, though; instead, I just changed the game again. I realized that soda was way too difficult to distribute without getting caught. I needed a more discreet product, so I switched to selling gum, which was actually much more profitable. I'd buy a pack with fifteen sticks in it and sell each of them for a dollar. I was making a 1,400 percent markup and getting fourteen dollars in profits basically every day.

I wasn't just wise about how I made money; I was wise about how I spent it too. In 1995, I was sixteen years old, and I bought my first car with the money I'd made shoveling snow and mowing lawns over a few summers. I met up with the owner with $2,500 in cash and proudly drove away in my 1985 white Honda CRX. Over the next few months, I was dead set on pimping out my ride, so I added new rims, tinted windows, and a killer sound system, but here's the thing: I did it all on my own. The point of all these stories is that, from a very young age, I looked for ways and means to save every penny I could. And over time, I built up enough savings to buy my own car.

It doesn't matter what you're saving up for; the secret to saving money is not waiting to save. It doesn't matter if you can afford to put away ten dollars or five hundred dollars a day—what matters is that you save and invest consistently over time. And the earlier you start, the better.

To put things in context, let's assume you stop in at Starbucks to grab a coffee every day on your commute. Sure, today you're only paying five dollars, but over the course of a year, you've spent $1,825 on coffee. That's kind of ridiculous. Say you wanted to save ten thousand dollars this year. It sounds intimidating if you're aiming to do it in one go. If you break it down, it's only twenty-seven dollars a day, which, by comparison, seems pretty reasonable. Your earning patterns should allow you to save a little bit of money each day, and over time, that will build your wealth.

In my second book, *Outsizing: Strategies to Grow Your Business, Profits, and Potential*, I mention how the patterns of our lives can have a strong influence on our outcomes. And our daily patterns will become evident over time if we stick to them. When I was in fifth grade, I got my first set of weights and started working out (most) days for the next thirty-four years. At forty-four years old, I'm now in the best shape of my life, and it's all because I established that pattern early on. I wouldn't have been able to build those muscles without the rhythm of daily behaviors. I'm not saying this to brag or suggest that everyone should start lifting weights before high school, because I'm sure a lot of people have gotten into much better shape much faster. Instead, I want to emphasize the idea that building something up over time also applies to how you save and invest your money.

✓ **CHECK YOURSELF**

Building your wealth takes time. It also takes discipline and intentional, repetitive behaviors. If you exercise your financial muscle regularly by saving and investing your money, you will achieve financial fitness. What are some ways you are exercising your financial muscle?

Building my earning potential

I've teased this several times, so I won't make you wait any longer to find out: How did I start my first proper business with *zero dollars*? Well, my rags-to-riches story started in the summer of 1994. I was fifteen years old, and at the time, I was working at my local Dairy Queen, flipping burgers and mixing Blizzards for $4.25 an hour. Even for the '90s, that was a spectacularly low wage. One day, a friend came in to grab a burger and saw me working in the kitchen. He waved me over, and we got to chatting a little. Then he said, "Hey, Steve, how would you like a job installing sprinkler systems?" At first, I had no idea what he was even talking about, as my family couldn't afford anything so fancy.

"What's a sprinkler system, Adam?" I asked.

"Underground sprinklers to water the lawn," he replied. "They'll pay you ten dollars an hour, and you can take your shirt off and get a tan—it'll be great."

I was sold. Shortly thereafter, I quit my job at Dairy Queen and spent the rest of the summer learning how to install sprinkler systems and working on my tan (because I *did* get to work shirtless). I was so much happier working outside, and I was eager to pick up that same gig the next summer in my junior year of high school. It was around May when I drove my car (now totally pimped out) down to the sprinkler shop to get my summer job back. I couldn't believe my eyes: The signs were gone, and the building was vacant. The yard that was once full of equipment was now empty, and there wasn't even a trace of the company I'd worked for only a year ago.

What do I do now? I thought. I desperately needed a summer job, and my plan was to keep installing sprinklers. Then it dawned on me: I didn't need a company to employ me over the summer; I'd just work for myself. I already knew how to install the sprinklers because I'd spent three months the previous summer busting my butt to learn everything I could about it. Being inquisitive and asking as many questions as possible of anyone who would answer me, I had obtained the skills I needed to do those jobs on my own. So, with those newly acquired skills and the strategy all those games of

Monopoly had taught me, I made some business cards for my own company, Steve's Sprinklers.

I displayed some of my business cards at the tanning salon where my sister worked, and almost immediately, people started hiring me. At first, it was just sprinklers, but as clients saw the quality of the work I'd done, I would get calls from client referrals about building patios, planting trees, and even installing retaining walls. I was smart about it, though. Instead of making ten dollars an hour when I worked on sprinkler systems, I charged fifty dollars an hour for my labor, plus the cost of the parts I had to buy, which I marked up 200 percent. Then, once I had built up enough of a reputation doing these "quick-fix" sprinkler service calls, I expanded to much bigger, more complicated landscaping projects. And for those fixed-price contracts, I would collect a deposit up front from clients for a portion of the project (say, twenty thousand dollars for a project that was going to cost fifty thousand), which gave me the working capital to buy the materials, pay for labor, and fund the expansion of my business.

It might sound like a lot, and at the time it seemed like a lot to me, too, because I was letting a scarcity mindset dictate my professional life and projecting the idea that *everyone* was financially insecure like I was. I quickly learned my worth, however, and I knew I was going to deliver the best quality work possible. Any skills I didn't have, I learned on the go, expanding my landscaping repertoire to suit the demand of my clients. As my reputation grew, more projects meant more money to advertise my business in local magazines and even the yellow pages (if you're too young to know what that means, ask your parents). From there, I had so much demand from so many clients that I needed to migrate from my makeshift office in my sister's garage to a proper business office. With that came more jobs, more money, and more opportunity to grow. Steve's Sprinklers quickly grew into a legitimate business that was employing friends and building some amazing projects. And that's how I started my first business with zero dollars.

Remember, I was only sixteen at the time, but I was conscious about investing in myself and in my own skills to maximize my earning potential. My focus wasn't on learning financial skills, but rather on developing communication skills, trust, integrity, and follow-through so I could liaise with clients, convince them I was the best one for the job, and then bring their vision to life and get a good endorsement for my next project. In addition to these life skills that weren't just relevant but necessary, I was dedicated to acquiring new skills related to design, installation, and landscaping so I would always be ten steps ahead of the competition.

Fast-forward about four years: I was two weeks shy of finishing the third year of my bachelor of science degree in business management. That's also when my education started becoming an obstacle to my career. I remember so clearly sitting in class, just a couple weeks away from finals, and feeling my phone buzzing nonstop in my pocket. I was getting inquiries and emails from new clients every few minutes asking if I could install their landscaping. The projects were getting bigger (and so were the paychecks), but so was the pressure on me to learn and develop new skills that would help me grow as quickly as my business. I realized at that moment that if I was going to have a great landscaping company, I couldn't let college get in the way of it.

I was straddling between being an entrepreneur and a student, and the situation was not sustainable, so I dropped out of school and pursued my company full time. Over the next decade, I put my heart and soul into the business. I rebranded the company to Superior Landscape Design—an award-winning design and build firm focused on building outdoor spaces with amenities like outdoor kitchens, fire and water features, putting greens, lighting, pools, pergolas, and other architectural elements—and watched it grow into a multimillion-dollar enterprise.

It would be another decade before I went back to school to finish my undergraduate degree, but the skills I'd gained in the meantime demonstrated my abilities better than any degree could have. I worked in an industry where people wanted to see results, not just proof that I'd gone to all my classes. Now, I'm definitely *not* saying you need to drop out of college if you want to be successful, but allow yourself the flexibility to take opportunities that may change your life's trajectory for the better. Turning my summer job into a successful landscaping company was an opportunity that paid off, but it came with sacrifices and years of hard work.

When I finally felt confident that my business was stable enough, I decided to go back to school to finish my undergraduate degree in accounting and finance. Business was booming, but I also was determined to finish my degree, so I learned to juggle clients with coursework. Over the next year, things were all going according to plan, and then, suddenly, they weren't. The 2008 global financial crash also brought with it a national housing market crisis that affected millions of homeowners. The financial crisis also meant a lot of uncertainty for construction and landscaping businesses. Within a matter of months, I went from being spoiled for choice when it came to new contracts to clients asking to put projects on hold and others asking for their deposits back entirely.

At that moment, I knew I had a choice to make: Do I persevere, or do I pivot? Fortunately, I was already committed to my plan of going back to school, so after a lot of deliberation, I made the difficult decision to walk away from the landscaping business and pursue something new. Like many other business owners, the financial crisis was a huge pivoting point for me. Running my own business was all I had known for the last decade, but as the economy spiraled, fewer people were building houses, and landscaping projects were drying up.

I'd spent the better part of thirteen years working on growing my side hustle into a successful business, and I was proud of what I'd accomplished, but I wanted to do something *different* now. Something more professional: a real white-collar, suit-and-tie career. But what?

Fortunately, I had developed a great relationship with other business owners and partners that I'd worked with on projects through my landscaping company, and I knew they needed help turning around *their* businesses. So, instead of going to work for someone else after I graduated, I set myself up as a freelance financial advisor and consulted with the business owners I knew to help their organizations grow into their full potential. Little did I know that my one-man freelance consultant gig would bloom into a full-fledged business. Starting my consulting firm Coltivar wasn't the end goal, though; it was only one part of an ever-evolving career plan.

By this time, I was thirty years old, married, had a family, and now had this new career I'd never even remotely planned for. I still wasn't *settled*, though. I'd learned the personal and professional skills to have a successful career, but I wanted to know more about the business side of running a company. I think on some level I had something to prove. I wanted to show myself that I was capable, that I could create my own successful business by showing other businesses how to be successful. So, I went back to school to get my MBA from the Fuqua School of Business at Duke University, and from there, I threw myself into growing Coltivar.

Fast-forward another few years: I was offered the CFO position for the construction and renewable energy company in Chattanooga I talked about in the previous chapter. The company had been around for almost fifty years and had hired me as a consultant to try and turn

things around and make them profitable again. After a year of consulting with me, they asked me to come on board, leaving me to answer
the same question again: Do I persevere, or do I pivot? I decided it
was time to pivot again, and I put things at Coltivar on hold. I didn't
shut down the company entirely, but I made plans to wrap up all the
projects we were currently working on, and I made sure my employees had other opportunities to pursue. Compared to when I walked
away from my landscaping company, this time I was better prepared
and better equipped to make sure I did right by my employees before
leaving. After laying off my employees and giving them all severance
packages, I packed up my house and my family, and we moved from
Denver across the country to start our next chapter.

And here's where things get a little bit heavy. Remember the job I
walked away from because it didn't align with my musts? This was it.

Turning around any company is a grueling and demanding task,
but this particular position was an incredibly lonely job because, in
every capacity, I felt like the outsider. The thing about being a CFO
and turnaround expert is that, regardless of the size and scope of the
problem you're dealing with, things almost always get worse before
they get better.

One night, after everyone had gone home for the day, I walked
alone down the halls of the empty office. As I walked along, I couldn't
help but notice how many employees had framed pictures of their
children or handmade drawings made by their kids displayed around
their offices. Pictures of families, smiling happily on vacation, camp-
ing trips, birthdays, you name it—these were snippets from their
lives *out there*, beyond this company. They were people with families
and lives beyond their jobs.

My heart lurched in my chest as I felt the weight of my responsibility. As a leader of this company, I was obligated to take care of
all these people—people who had no idea just how bad the situation

was or how chaotic things were behind the scenes. Making major decisions that would impact an entire company was an unimaginably challenging period of my life, and that responsibility weighed on me in a big way. Ultimately, that job didn't allow me to share my unique abilities, particularly when it came to being a positive, empathetic light or an influence for good on the people around me. Despite being good at my job, the work I was doing wasn't honoring myself or reflecting my musts, and that's how I knew I had to reevaluate my career. I was able to learn some valuable lessons through that position, though, but not in the way you might expect.

As part of the new job, I attended a CFO accelerator program at the MIT Sloan School of Management in Boston. The course largely focused on how to build strategic skills as a CFO and how to be an effective leader within a growing company. Becoming a CFO had never been part of my plan, so just as I'd done with my summer sprinkler job at sixteen, I used this as an opportunity to learn as much as I could. Out of nearly a dozen speakers, the one who stood out to me was a visiting professor from the Wharton School of the University of Pennsylvania. He gave a talk about fintech, which is basically how businesses utilize new technology to compete with more traditional methods of delivering financial services to customers. The professor went on to discuss how the business world was evolving toward a focus on technology, coding, and data analytics. I was busy taking notes when he said something that made me stop and think: "Don't try to learn the skills the world needs today. Build the skills the world will demand in ten to fifteen years." It felt like he was talking directly to me. I thought I was there to learn how to do the best job in my current career as a CFO, but those words stuck out to me so much that I actually felt a shift in my focus from where I was at that moment to where I wanted to be in fifteen years.

Over the next few years, I dedicated time to expanding my tech skills. I learned how to develop software and how to understand data analytics, and I went on to start a second company, a strategy management software called Mativ. I was on a mission to keep learning, continue developing new, relevant skills, and maintain a mindset that was open to opportunities to evolve.

It's important to always be aware of how the world around you is changing and use that information to anticipate the best position for you to be in when that change happens. That means allowing yourself to evolve, update your skills, or learn different ones. The best business owners aren't the ones that remain static; they're the ones that have the vision to stay ahead of the change, plan for what services the world is going to require, and learn how they can deliver the best version of those services. You've probably heard the expression, "Give someone a fish and he'll eat for a day; teach him to fish and he'll eat for a lifetime." Well, I like to take that one step further and say, why not teach people how to build fishing poles? Give them the skills to start their own business and build relationships with people who sell the materials to build fishing poles. Then, provide them with learning opportunities so they can grow their business to meet the evolving needs of people in their community and bless their own life and the lives of those around them.

A successful business ultimately isn't determined by how much money it earns; it's determined by how well you're able to adapt your business strategy and integrate new information so you're always maximizing its earning potential. Along with investing in yourself so you have the skills to do that, being financially literate is essential to being financially fit overall. We've already covered this, but after I'd grown my side-hustle summer job into a sizable landscape company, I still had no idea how to read a financial statement. Sure, I could look at the numbers in the different columns and infer what they represented, but I had very little knowledge about how to understand the story behind the numbers. I needed to learn the cause and effect of what the numbers meant and then use that knowledge to execute effective changes. For example, before I became financially literate, seeing that our gross margin was down by 20 percent just meant bad news, but I had no understanding of why or how I could fix it. With the skills to read and interpret financial statements, I could look at the same report and know it meant I needed to review things like pricing or where I could utilize technology to streamline our processes and drive greater efficiency in the field.

If you think that doesn't apply to you because you aren't gung-ho about starting your own business, financial literacy also applies to your personal life. It's particularly important when it comes to how you invest. Making sure you have a working knowledge of finance will give you the upper hand when it comes to investing wisely, as well as the confidence to invest in specific stocks or other financial instruments without being weaseled out of your money by financial advisors who charge you excessive fees to do something you could probably do for yourself. So, financial literacy skills aren't just for the business CEOs; they're also important for the average Joe (and Jane).

Another important distinction when it comes to earning potential is the difference between living off wages and living off capital. One of the hard truths of life is that it is extremely difficult (not impossible, but unlikely) to build true wealth by working for somebody else. If you do live off wages, chances are you're investing some of those wages into businesses by buying stock for big companies you believe in, and that's how you make passive income (if you choose the stocks wisely). Alternatively, you might invest in yourself and start a business that produces assets you sell, and then you live off the capital generated by that cash flow. Either way, the earlier you start putting money aside (preferably into investments that have big opportunities to grow), the better. And the more time you invest in learning skills like understanding finance and how you can maximize your ability to live off capital, the more freedom you'll have to live that lifestyle you were planning for.

I've come a long way from playing my own version of Monopoly to having several multimillion-dollar companies, and it wasn't an easy road by any means. I believe that anyone who makes a concerted effort to understand what it takes to be financially fit has the capability to do the same. Learning how to take what you already have and use it to maximize your earning potential depends on your ability to *act* with discipline and intention, *think* with the intention to know when to persevere and when to pivot, and above all else, *invest*—in yourself, in your skills, and in your future.

🧠 Exercise Your Knowledge

Here are five questions to ask yourself to better understand your current and future earning potential. Remember, the more honest you are in answering these questions, the better chance you'll have at successfully improving your financial fitness.

- How does your current level of education, skills, and experience affect your earning potential now?
- What are some opportunities you may need to pursue to increase your earning potential in future?
- What does the future of your current career field look like?
- How can you prepare to align your own professional trajectory to complement the needs of that field in ten to fifteen years?
- What can you do today to prepare yourself for growing your earning potential through passive income tomorrow?

CHAPTER 9

Spending

L et's assume you have applied what you've learned about planning and earning to your own life. You've dedicated time to developing your go-forward plan, identified resources and skills you need to achieve your goals, and figured out how to improve your earning potential. Great! Now, how do you handle spending what you earn?

> **Lightbulb Moment:** How you spend your money is arguably more important than how you earn it when it comes to your financial fitness. Regardless of whether you make $50,000 a year, $150,000 a year, or even $500,000 a year, it's possible to "out-lifestyle" your income. And that's just a fancy way of saying "spending more than you earn" or spending beyond your means.

Spending outside your needs

There are two fundamental errors I see people make when it comes to how they spend their money, and both hinder their ability to become financially fit. The first mistake people make is spending outside of their *needs*. Frivolous spending can occur for any number of reasons, but most are rooted in the underlying need to *feel* something. We might spend money because we're bored and need something new to get excited about, or we want to feel more important, or look more impressive. Perhaps we just think buying nicer clothes or a newer car will make us feel more secure about our life. Whatever the reason is, this type of spending is due to our susceptibility and impulsivity, and it leads to fleeting feelings of happiness and fulfillment.

✓ CHECK YOURSELF

Even though the feelings we get from frivolous spending don't endure, the desire to satisfy our egos is what makes the world economy go round. In fact, advertising is such a lucrative endeavor that North American businesses spend almost $300 billion each year selling ad space. We are constantly subliminally primed to want to spend our money. On average, we see between four thousand and ten thousand ads every single day. So, it's pretty easy for you to decide what to spend your money on; you just look around or check social media—there are literally thousands of options right at your fingertips. And before you know it, you've just spent half of your income on stuff you don't even need (or particularly want). Unfortunately, when it comes to spending, learning to control your ego can be a difficult thing to do. It's not impossible, though.

If you feel like it's difficult to control your ego when it

comes to spending, consider your behavior when you make purchases. In particular, ask yourself *why* you're making a purchase. Is it impulsive? Are you doing it to keep up with others or to earn someone else's respect? When we engage in ego-driven spending, we often do so at the cost of our genuine needs and financial goals. So, by being intentional with spending and finding fulfillment beyond material possessions, we can lead a more financially responsible and fulfilling life.

Getting your financial house in order starts with identifying your values. Just as knowing what your personal musts are for your go-forward plan, being aware of what you value plays an important role in setting yourself up for financial success. Once you've identified the values you hold yourself to, you can examine how your spending honors those values or how it *doesn't*.

James Clear, the author of *Atomic Habits*, has dedicated a lot of time to understanding human behavior when it comes to decision-making. Although Clear has identified almost sixty possible core values—from authenticity and creativity to wisdom and leadership—that we can use to shape how we live our lives, he emphasizes that it's important to focus on just four or five when thinking about which values apply to us personally.

Remember that your values and your musts aren't inherently the same thing. They can overlap in some ways or reflect the same moral or ethical standards you want to personify in your life, but values are often flexible for some people (although they shouldn't be). For example, you can value your health but rely on getting takeout most nights of the week because it's more convenient. Or perhaps you value honesty and openness, but the fear of confrontation or potential conflict may hold you back from fully expressing yourself in relationships. On the other hand, your musts are your absolutes, the beliefs and practices you cannot waver on. When thinking about your values, it's essential to reflect on what they mean to you personally and how they align with your life's purpose. Ask yourself how these values can influence your actions, decisions, and interactions with others and how they reflect your most authentic self. For example, in my own life, I recognize that kindness helps foster strong connections and a positive impact on those around me. I also value creativity, and that fuels my passion for problem-solving and innovation. By prioritizing these values and allowing them to shape my decisions and choices, I'm able to live a life that reflects these values and connects back to my higher purpose.

Exercise Your Knowledge

Once you've identified your values, grab a copy of your latest bank or credit card statement and label each item you spent money on according to the value it serves. Do your most treasured values correlate to your biggest expenses? Are you spending little or nothing on the things you value the most?

Spending beyond your means

Staying true to spending on what you really value allows you to spend with purpose and avoid spending simply to satisfy yourself (or others). Purpose-driven spending is also crucial because it can prevent you from making the second big spending mistake, which is spending outside of your *means*. This refers to spending more money than you can afford, either by buying things on credit or spending beyond your budget on things that don't necessarily honor your musts. When you continuously spend more money than you have, you create a subsequent borrowing problem by incurring all kinds of unnecessary debt (we talk more about borrowing in chapter 10).

Sometimes, we aren't even aware that we're spending unnecessarily. Getting to the root of overspending takes strategy and emotional awareness, because spending isn't just about finance, it's about psychology too. This is particularly true for young people who experience social pressure and feel like they have to keep up with portraying a specific lifestyle image on social media by spending money on lavish vacations and activities. In these cases, *not* spending actually feels more dire than creating debt that they'll need to pay back later. In reality, though, if you out-lifestyle your income while you're young, you're setting up your future self to be financially unfit. On the other hand, if you practice spending primarily on what you need and budget for the things you want (like the vacation or the fancy dinners), you can home in on the purpose of your spending, which will help you gauge whether it's worth parting with your hard-earned income and make future you happier in the long run.

In addition, budgeting empowers us to make mindful and purposeful decisions about how we use our financial resources, which helps us make sure we're living in alignment with our values and creating a life that reflects what matters most to us. Even though it might feel tedious or like an unnecessary effort, by creating a values-based budget, we can prioritize expenses that reflect those values and cut back on unnecessary or ego-driven spending. Ultimately, by being intentional with our money, we can lead a more fulfilling life that reflects our core values.

Exercise Your Knowledge

By honestly assessing your spending habits and understanding the underlying reasons for overspending, you can take proactive steps to bring your budget back in line with your values and financial aspirations. With awareness and intentionality, you can create a more mindful and fulfilling relationship with your finances. Take some time to review your recent spending habits and consider the following questions:

1. *Where are you spending beyond your means?* Look at your expenses and identify areas where you consistently overspend or go over your budget.

2. *What are the reasons behind your overspending?* Reflect on why you tend to spend more in those specific areas. Is it due to ego-driven purchases, trying to keep up with others, or seeking validation through material possessions?

3. *How do these spending habits align with your values and financial goals?* Consider whether these spending patterns reflect what truly matters to you and whether they contribute to your long-term financial well-being.

4. *Try to identify what emotions or triggers lead to this type of spending.* Pay attention to situations or emotions that tempt you to overspend and consider whether you need to spend time reframing or reevaluating what money means to you and whether these patterns will hurt or hinder your ideal financial future.

CHAPTER 10

Borrowing

t feels like I've been talking a lot about money over the last few chapters. So, to shake things up, let's talk about the opposite of money: debt.

> 💡 **Lightbulb Moment:** For such a small word, *debt* can be an incredibly intimidating, even overwhelming subject to think about. For most people, reducing their debt is something they think about at least once a month, usually when it's time to pay their credit card bill.

To put things in context, at the beginning of 2023, the average American owed roughly $96,700.[1] Across the pond, the average Brit owed about half that amount: $42,000.[2] Accumulating debt is incredibly easy, especially if you're living beyond your needs and means, but getting rid of it is infinitely more difficult. Why? Well, there are several reasons.

The main reason is because most people (43 percent to be exact)[3] only pay the minimum balance due when they pay their bill—either because that's all they can afford to pay or because they are only looking at their monthly payment and not the long-term overall costs.

Another reason is because the world economy has evolved into a digital conglomerate of intangible (if not completely invisible) finance. It's effortless to spend money when you can't see it leaving your bank account. However, when you've got a finite number of bills in your wallet that you can see disappearing as you spend them, *how* you spend becomes much more nuanced.

For example, in 2013, Disneyland theme parks revolutionized the way consumers enjoy the "happiest place on earth" by changing one crucial thing: going digital. Guests now wore rubber wristbands encoded with credit card information to help streamline ticket checks and concession sales and even make waiting in line less tedious. From then on, running out of cash was a nonissue because you could buy overpriced snacks and gimmicky souvenirs with the swish of your wrist. Don't get me wrong, Disneyland is one of my favorite places on earth, but this story demonstrates just how intangible spending money has become and how quickly we can spend more than we plan to.

When I was just starting out in the business world, writing a check was a powerful reminder of how much I was spending. Writing out the words *one hundred and forty-five dollars* made me think more deeply about the consequences of my spending. Now, a little over two decades later, I'm sitting in bed, buying a new phone charger online with the push of a button, even though I've already got two. It's an incredibly convenient, dangerously slippery spending slope.

But it's not just people like me who have adjusted swiftly into the age of artificial money. Kids are unknowingly making purchases via iPads and iPhones without realizing what they're doing. In fact, Apple has paid out tens of millions of dollars in lawsuits filed by parents of children who have racked up serious bills of unauthorized in-app purchases.[4] Even my own children fall victim to the scam of using real money to buy fake stuff. For Christmas and her birthday, my daughter asks for gift cards so that she can buy clothes for her character on Roblox (an online interactive gaming platform). Of course, I oblige her because I know it makes her happy, but in my head, I'm thinking what a scam it is to encourage children to spend money buying something in the virtual world rather than something they can touch and play with in real life. An entire generation is handling artificial money before they can even comprehend what exactly they're spending it on. By the end of the month, all that effortless spending has racked up hundreds, if not thousands, of dollars in credit card debt. And while it can be dangerous to not see the money we have, not being able to keep track of all the money we *owe* in debts is arguably more harmful to our financial fitness.

Closely related to only paying the minimum due, another reason debt is so difficult to get rid of is *interest*. "Buy now, pay later" schemes are deceptively enticing. However, at the end of the day, they exist to help banks make money from buyers. They do this by collecting more interest when it takes buyers a long time to pay it off. Black Friday is a great example of companies taking advantage of consumers' willingness to buy using credit cards. Big ticket items you ordinarily wouldn't spend money on are discounted to entice you to spend on things you don't need—because if you don't, you're missing out on a huge opportunity, right? Not necessarily.

Let's say you buy a $1,500 item for 20 percent off (it now costs $1,200, if you want to skip the mental math). You don't have that in cash, so you choose to pay it by putting it on your credit card. It seems like a great deal: You get to enjoy the item now, and future you gets stuck figuring out the bill. There's a catch, though: Each credit card payment comes with a 15 percent annual interest fee that is computed daily. If you pay off the credit card by making thirty-five-dollar monthly payments, it will take you forty-six months to pay down the balance, and you'll spend $376 in interest, which works out to be more than you would have spent in the first place if you bought the item at full price. Crazy, right?

When it comes to debt, my advice is this: If you're able, pay back your debt as quickly as reasonably possible. I'm not saying you should eat rice and beans for dinner every night so you can pay off your mortgage, but you'll be in a much better financial position if you're able to invest some of the money you save by paying off that interest quicker. The caveat here is that in some circumstances, paying off asset-based debt (particularly debt that has a low interest rate and is producing cash flow) isn't always the best option. What I mean is that by immediately paying off low-interest debt tied to an asset, like a rental property, you could overlook or miss out on the potential for higher returns from other investment opportunities (say, buying a second rental property). Using all your money to pay back debt could limit the opportunity that comes from using leverage to invest in asset-based debt. I'm not saying you should go out and get yourself into a bunch of asset-based debt, however; it's crucial to assess your individual financial situation first. The take-home message here is that it's possible to utilize debt to your advantage, and a balanced approach that weighs debt repayment against investment potential can ultimately lead you to a more financially sound strategy.

✓ CHECK YOURSELF

Although this chapter has focused on the dangers of debt and how to avoid it wherever possible, it would be incomplete without mentioning that there is actually such a thing as good debt. Acquiring certain types of debt may be necessary and even essential to your success financially. The difference between good debt and bad debt is that good debt is used to buy assets, which produce income, while bad debt is used to buy liabilities, which result in more expenses. Liabilities include things like buying cars and houses, while assets might include things like a rental property or a vehicle you're going to use to start your own company (like I did with Steve's Sprinklers). Typically, people who are financially fit and understand the importance of financial literacy not only understand how these types of debt are fundamentally different, but they also know how to utilize good debt to their advantage.

Paying off debt

The reality is that for a majority of people, incurring debt through purchasing things that aren't strictly assets (like debt from a mortgage or even student loans) is pretty common. As a side note, there's a lot of debate over whether buying a house is the good kind of debt or whether it is more of a liability, and the short answer is that it will depend on your unique financial situation. In particular, a home might be seen as more of a liability than an asset because of the ongoing expenses and financial responsibilities that come with owning it. While a home can give you a place to live and possibly increase in value, you'll also have to pay for things like the mortgage, property taxes, insurance, and repairs. These costs really start to add up and become a significant burden if you're not prepared. Plus, a lot of your money will be tied up in the house, which means you might miss out on other investment opportunities that could bring higher returns. So, depending on your financial situation, a home might be more of a long-term financial commitment rather than a simple way to acquire an asset that will make your money back in the future.

Unfortunately, figuring out how to pay debt down as quickly as possible can get overwhelming. If that applies to you, don't panic! When it comes to paying off debt, especially if it's debt you've incurred through purchasing liabilities, how you choose to pay it off can make a *huge* difference.

One approach to paying off your debt is to use the snowball method. When using this method, you make the minimum payments on all of your debts and put a little extra money toward the *smallest* balance of debt. Once that debt is paid off, you then move on to paying off the one with the next smallest debt. The benefit of using this method is that you can pay off smaller debts more quickly, and seeing that steady progress will drive you to keep paying off your debts. So, each time you eliminate one balance of debt, it's like a psychological win that keeps you motivated.

The alternative is to start by paying off the debt with the highest interest rate *first*. This is called the avalanche method. With this method, you make the minimum payment on all of your debts and then put any extra money toward the one with the highest interest rate. As you may have guessed, once that debt is paid off, you move on to the next highest one, using the same method to pay off that debt, and so on. The benefit of using this method is that by paying off the debt with the highest interest rate first, you'll actually save money in the long run. So, while you don't get the benefit of seeing debts get paid off quickly, this strategy is best if you're looking for a financial win.

A third option for paying off debt is through something called *interest rate arbitrage*. This method involves using a secondary credit facility that has a lower interest rate to pay off a debt with a higher interest rate more imminently. For example, if you have debt from a student loan that has a 7 percent interest rate, but you have a credit card that will give you zero percent interest on charges for a year, you could use the credit card to pay interest on the student loan for twelve months to reduce the amount of interest you owe.

Keep in mind that there is no strictly right or wrong option when it comes to paying off debt, because ultimately the method you choose to use will depend on your personal preferences, financial situation, and short- and long-term goals. However, unless you have no other options, borrowing from your future self (assuming you are using debt to acquire a liability rather than an asset) is a huge no-no when it comes to financial fitness, and if you can avoid it by spending smartly, you should. Again, my primary advice on debt is to avoid it wherever possible and pay it back as fast as is reasonable for your individual circumstances.

A major scientific study about financial strategies found that people who were financially stressed due to overspending experienced greater physical health complications, interpersonal relationship struggles, and even a more anxious retirement.[5] That's *astounding*. Not only is acquiring debt bad for your financial fitness, but it can also negatively impact your quality of life. On the flip side, people who were in control of their spending experienced greater fulfillment and a more positive, happier life. Similar to the study I mentioned in chapter 2 about income and happiness, this study gives us insight into the power of smart spending and minimizing how much we're borrowing from our future self. I know which type of person I want to be. Do you?

Exercise Your Knowledge

Here are a few questions to help you feel less overwhelmed when it comes to dealing with your debt. Remember, this exercise isn't about judging or criticizing yourself for having debt. Rather, it's an opportunity to reflect on and assess which debts are asset-based or liability-based and then consider different debt repayment strategies that can help you create a more informed and effective plan for managing your debts.

1. *Identify your debts*. Make a list of all your debts, such as credit card balances, student loans, car loans, and mortgage.

2. *Determine if they are asset-based or liability-based.* Categorize each debt as either asset-based or liability-based. Remember, asset-based debts produce income and ultimately cash flow (e.g., an investment property or business) and contribute to your overall financial well-being. Liability-based debts result in expenses and ultimately reduce your cash flow, and they also take away from your financial resources and don't contribute to long-term wealth (e.g., consumer credit cards or cars).

3. *Prioritize debt repayment.* Assess how you are prioritizing paying off your debts. Are you focusing on high-interest debts first, or do you have a different approach?

4. *Consider debt payoff strategies.* Reflect on different methods of paying off debts, such as the snowball method (starting with the smallest debt first) or the avalanche method (tackling high-interest debts first). Which approach might work best for your financial situation and goals?

5. *Evaluate the impact on your financial freedom.* Bring it back to your long-term vision and consider how reducing or eliminating certain debts might increase your financial freedom and provide more flexibility in achieving your long-term objectives.

Understanding how to prioritize your debt repayment can lead to a path of improved financial well-being and greater control over your financial future.

CHAPTER 11

Investing

K nowing when, where, and how to invest your money can be an intimidating prospect, but it doesn't need to be. In fact, part of my overarching goal is to make sure that investing isn't overwhelming. It doesn't matter what position you're currently in: a stay-at-home parent, a working professional with a sturdy 401(k), or a recent college grad. I want you to be confident that you deserve the opportunity to grow your finances through genuine investment strategies. I also want you to understand which investment death traps to avoid so you can build lasting value and lifelong wealth.

> **Lightbulb Moment:** It's important to recognize that money is a language, and globally, less than 30 percent of the population is financially literate.[1] This isn't really surprising, considering that financial concepts aren't usually taught in schools, which means that children grow up not understanding finance in any great detail and basically have to navigate the economic road map while wearing a metaphorical blindfold.

continued

This has significant effects on day-to-day life, including how much money they earn and save, how much debt they incur, and how much interest they pay.

Investing wisely

From a business perspective, not understanding the language of money or not being financially literate impacts things like profits and returns on capital and overall business value. The good news? You don't need to become the CEO of a huge company to achieve a financially abundant life. There are a number of small decisions you can make today that will change your life in the long run. When it comes to making wise investment decisions, there are two critical oversights I frequently observe: incurring excessive fees and failing to maximize returns. These oversights have the potential to significantly impact your long-term financial success. It is essential for you to be mindful of these factors in order to achieve your goals.

As a warm-up, I want to take you through a simple example that demonstrates the profound impact of excessive fees. Let's assume you have $100,000 you want to invest at 8 percent over the next thirty years. You have the choice of whether to invest in a low-cost index fund, which charges 0.05 percent in fees, or an actively managed fund that charges 2 percent in fees. While 2 percent might seem like a miniscule charge, over the next thirty years, the extra 1.95 percent in fees that you'd be paying in an actively managed fund would cost you an extra $317,000 on your investment. Those small fees add up at the end of the day and ultimately will lead to you working longer to earn the same amount of money.

When it comes to investing in assets and maximizing returns, there are a number of things you can invest in, such as cash, bonds, real estate, equities (stocks), or a business. Let's take that $100,000 from the preceding example and talk about where the money actually goes while it grows. Where you invest your money will determine how much you make back over that thirty-year period. Cash will yield the lowest payoff (roughly 1 percent per year) and will likely not be a worthwhile investment as the value of cash decreases thanks to inflation. If you choose to invest your money in bonds or real estate, you'll likely see a less than 10 percent increase in your money per year over thirty years and around a 10 percent increase per year if you invest in equities over the same period. On the other hand, if you take that $100,000 and invest it in a business, and you're able to drive that business to its full potential through expanding and growing your profits on capital, adjusting for demand, and preparing for obstacles, you may be able to achieve a greater than 20 percent return year over year on your business's value.

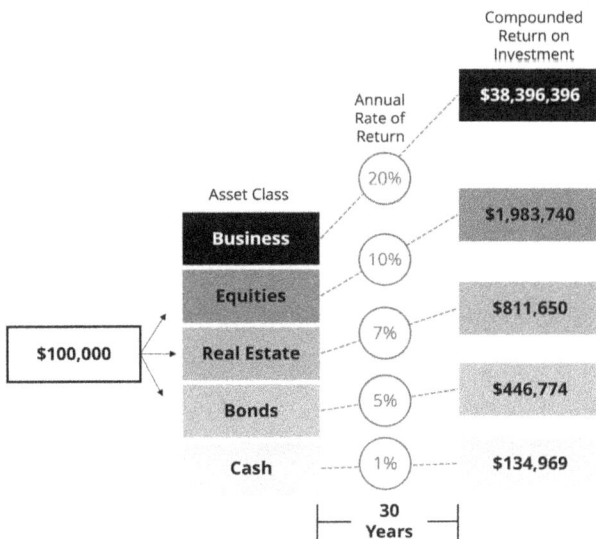

Figure 11.1. This demonstrates how investing $100,000 over thirty years across different asset classes, including cash, bonds, real estate, equities, and business, with varying rates of returns, can result in significantly divergent financial outcomes.

✓ **CHECK YOURSELF**

How can you determine which assets will be a worthwhile investment ahead of time? One rule of thumb is called the rule of 72. You can use this rule to calculate how long it will take you to double your money. Simply take 72 and divide it by the average annual interest rate you'll receive on your investment. For example, let's assume you receive 7 percent per year on your investments. If you divide 72 by 7, you get 10.3, which is the number of years it would take an investment earning 7 percent per year to double.

The language of investing

When it comes to investing in financial assets, it's crucial to be well-informed about the potential risks involved. Market volatility, economic downturns, and unexpected events all can impact the value of your investments. So, it's smart to stay alert and consider these factors when making investment decisions.

Another risk is paying too much for an asset by not understanding what factors actually drive its intrinsic value or underlying worth based on the sum of its future cash flows. For instance, some people speculate and gamble by picking the hottest stocks without paying attention to the fundamental economics behind them. It's important to understand that a combination of factors—such as strong financial performance, reliable cash flows, a solid competitive advantage, and future growth prospects—drive the value of a stock. By grasping the language of investing, you can avoid overpaying for an asset or investing in one that won't generate optimal returns.

If you're investing in your own business, you need to consider things like the efficacy of your strategy and whether you understand the value drivers of your business and how to implement them effectively and in a timely manner. Bad investment decisions (which are a direct consequence of financial illiteracy) can affect both business owners and average investors. If you're an average investor, not understanding basic financial concepts may cost you in excessive fees and subpar performance. From a business perspective, not being financially literate can erode your investment returns by preventing you from understanding and pursuing the proper business strategy that will lead you to financial abundance.

Investing in your own business isn't for everyone, and that's okay. What do your best options look like then? When it comes to investing in equities, like the stock market for example, the worst possible strategy is to have your money sitting in cash.

You may be wondering, *Is now a good time?* Especially as I'm writing this book during a period of great economic uncertainty, a lot of people are wondering whether to wait to invest in case there's a recession. The truth is that recessions happen cyclically, but so does the uptick in gross domestic product growth that we see after every market contraction. When it comes to investing in stocks, it's time *in* the market, not *timing* the market that matters. Especially if you're new to investing, it's important to keep in mind the dangers of "sitting on the sidelines." By that, I mean not participating in investing your money in stocks or other assets. I realize that some people might feel hesitant or scared to invest because they're worried about uncertainty—or worse, losing their money—but I guarantee you that by staying on the sidelines with a bunch of cash and continuing to not invest it, you'll miss out on potential opportunities to grow your money and build wealth over time through the power of compound interest. Even if you don't think you can invest a "meaningful" amount in the stock market right now, remember that the opportunity to invest a dollar today makes it more valuable than a dollar you'll earn tomorrow. In other words, if you wait until you think you have enough money to invest, it'll be too late for you to see that money grow significantly over your lifetime.

Through small means, great things can come to pass. Get started now!

This chart illustrates, with the power of compounding interest, how much money you would have if you invested consistently over time.

Monthly investment	After 10 years	After 20 Years	After 30 Years
$100	$17.3K	$54.9K	$135.9K
$250	$43.5K	$137.3K	$339.8K
$500	$86.9K	$274.6K	$679.7K
$1,000	$173.8K	$549.1K	$1.4M

Assumes an average 8.0% annual return.

SITTING ON THE SIDELINES

The annual growth rate of the S&P 500 from 1996 to 2015 was

8.2%

Let's see what would happen if you missed out on the top trading days during this period.

If you missed...	You would realize...
Top **10** trading days	8.2% → **4.5%**
Top **20** trading days	8.2% → **2.1%**
Top **30** trading days	8.2% → **0.0%**

Figure 11.2. By sitting on the sidelines and not investing, you could miss out on substantial gains over time through the power of compound interest.

Whether you're planning on growing your own business or looking for companies to invest in, as I mentioned, it's important to consider the business *value*. Lots of things drive business value—strategy, specialization, employees, skills—and as the investor, your investment drives cash flow, which drives value too. But you can't just go throwing money blindly into hot-topic stocks without understanding the story behind their free cash flow. Free cash flow is the amount of cash generated by a company after deducting all expenses and investments needed to maintain or expand its business operations. It represents the cash available for distribution to investors, debt repayment, or reinvestment. Whether you're investing in stocks, bonds, real estate, a business, or something else, what you're *actually* investing in is the promise of cash you're going to be given from making that specific investment. Warren Buffett (you didn't think I was going to get through the entire chapter on investing without mentioning him, did you?) emphasizes that the only real way to evaluate the value of something is through figuring out its intrinsic value. That value reflects the total value of all the future cash flow that a business's assets will produce over its remaining life. That might sound a little technical, so let's break it down with a simple example using one of the oldest businesses in the book: the humble lemonade stand.

Hypothetically, let's say I own a lemonade stand that makes one dollar in cash every year (*not profits*—that's an important distinction). After five years, the lemonade stand is going to have produced five dollars in cash. Now, if I want to sell that lemonade stand to you, how much would you be prepared to pay? At face value, it isn't worth more than five dollars. If you think buying the business from me is a risky investment, you might be willing to pay me three dollars, but if you know the business will make at least five dollars over the next five years and you come in with a great investment mindset and a plan to grow the business and increase that cash from one dollar to twenty dollars a year, you might be willing to pay me a little more than five dollars. Investing works exactly the same way. It doesn't matter how elaborate or simplistic the assets you're investing in are; what you should be focused on is knowing how much cash they can produce over their lifetime.

If you do own a business, here's my advice: Don't just play to play; play to win. Across a majority of industries—tech, construction, hospitality, healthcare—10 percent of companies own two-thirds of the economic profits. Plan to do the best you can; give yourself opportunities to learn more about the financial drivers of business in your industry and then learn the skills to apply those drivers to your production. For businesses, value is created at the intersection of finance and strategy.

Remember, money is a language you can learn to speak at any age. The majority of the world still hasn't learned this skill—don't let yourself be one of those people. Investing in yourself and harnessing the power to manage your own finances are key steps to growing your wealth. By taking control of your investment decisions, you can unlock the potential for long-term financial success. I'm not saying that working with financial advisors is a bad thing; just don't rely solely on others to make all of your financial decisions for you. Instead, empower yourself to make informed choices that align with your goals and values. By investing time in educating yourself about the stock market, understanding different investment strategies, and seeking out opportunities for growth, you can pave the way to a prosperous financial future. Remember, generating wealth doesn't happen overnight. It requires dedication, patience, and continuous learning. So, seize the opportunity to invest in yourself and reap the rewards of financial independence.

Exercise Your Knowledge

Prepare to make your own investments by creating a mock investment portfolio. Start with selecting a group of stocks or other investments from companies you think are valuable now or will be more valuable in the future. Track their performance over a set period, say, six months. At the end of the period, compare how your mock portfolio did compared to other stocks in the broader market. Actively practicing your investment plans not only helps you learn more about investing, risk management, and performance tracking, but it will allow you to experience what it would be like to invest—without risking any of your actual money.

CHAPTER 12

Giving

Successful people give their money, time, and talent to causes greater than themselves. That doesn't mean you need to donate all your money to charity to be successful, but when we give, we are tapping into our greater human purpose, which is to abundantly bless the lives of those around us.

> **Lightbulb Moment:** You may be thinking, *Steve, you've just told me how I can earn all this money and now you're telling me I need to give it away?* It sounds counterintuitive that you need to give in order to become financially fit, but the psychology behind generosity demonstrates why giving is such an important part of the financial fitness model.

Think back to when I said that if we view money as the object of our satisfaction, we will never feel satisfied. If we want to be truly satisfied, we must view money as a tool to bless ourselves and others. When we engage in prosocial spending (i.e., spending on others rather than ourselves), our brains are rewarded with the release of hormones like oxytocin and endorphins, which makes us feel good.

That's not even the interesting part, though. Studies have shown that the level of happiness people feel when they donate actually isn't correlated with the size of their donation. That means that someone who is able to give more won't feel happier than someone who's able to give less. It's biology's way of leveling the financial playing field so everyone can feel good when they do good. You might think you're currently not in a place to donate a meaningful amount, but even if it's a small amount, seeing the positive impact of giving is more rewarding (physiologically speaking) than keeping or receiving money for yourself.

Most religious groups abide by some form of tithing. Specifically, in an ecclesiastical practice, the rule is to give 10 percent of your income to the church to support its mission and work to help those who need it. The idea behind tithing is that all of the earth's resources were created by God or a higher power, and therefore what we have isn't ours to keep in the first place. Thus, by giving a portion of our income back to God through a church, we are demonstrating our faith in God's abundance and acting to bless the lives of others.

I have seen tithing bless my life in miraculous ways. First, by giving away a portion of my money, I stay true to my purpose to elevate the lives of others through the talents and resources with which I have been gifted. Plus, tithing helps me to remain humble and disciplined when it comes to spending. I've witnessed countless examples of people who can barely cover their financial obligations but who consistently pay their tithes, and before they knew it, they were blessed with better jobs, more opportunities to earn money, greater capacities to save money, and circumstances that helped them to avoid financial losses. There is power in giving.

Giving your time

Giving doesn't necessarily have to mean donating money to a church or other nonprofit organization. In fact, you can give *without* spending any money at all. Giving your time or donating your skills to enriching the lives of those around you will allow you to feel just as fulfilled.

If you're unable to spend money on what you love, make an effort to dedicate time to the things you're passionate about and be conscious about making sure your behaviors align with your values. That might include spending time improving your relationships with the people in your life—partners, children, parents, siblings, friends, or whoever matters to you most—because I guarantee you, it will be difficult to make money (or hold on to the money you have) if you don't make an effort to work on strained relationships.

Take my own experience, for example. I was so focused on work that my job became a distraction from the things I was struggling with in my personal life. It didn't matter how much time I spent learning how to be financially literate or how closely I followed my go-forward plan. Not even the six drivers of financial fitness could prepare me for the financial consequences of getting divorced. Obviously, dividing up our collective assets and finances didn't come as a surprise to me, and I was the one who ultimately made the choice to leave. But after all the sacrifices I had made to get to that position only to end up with half of what I'd spent years building up, I realized an important lesson. I should have been more intentional with my time, and I should have given myself more grace to take care of the relationships that were important to me. Would I have worked through things in my marriage if I'd given more time to that relationship? Not necessarily. But shared custody means I only get half the time I would have had with my kids. What I'm trying to say is that at the end of the day, it doesn't matter how much money you have in savings or how big your house is; if you have no one to share it with, that is true scarcity.

I know people who are so caught up in their careers they don't make time to speak to their children regularly. If we aren't conscious about the example we set for our children, they may grow up to resent us or feel neglected, and they are more likely to develop emotional and social struggles of their own. In turn, you might need to pay for things like therapy or rehab (either for yourself or your children), and that ends up costing you both time and money. It also might distract you from doing well at your own job, and so the spiral continues. It's an extreme example, but it does highlight how giving our time to the people and things that are important to us can be more valuable than money.

✓ CHECK YOURSELF

Giving of yourself is essential, whether through supporting a charity you're passionate about or by donating your time and energy to taking care of yourself and your loved ones. If you fail to give, it will end up costing you in the long run—emotionally, physiologically, socially, and maybe even financially. So, before you embark on your financial fitness transformation, recognize that, unlike the amount of money you can make, time is finite and how you spend it matters.

Giving to yourself

First and foremost, though, before you pay your bills or your mortgage or donate money to causes, give to yourself. Here, I actually am referring to money. Make sure that when you get the opportunity, you squirrel away or invest savings for your future self. For example, I set up automatic transfers that occur every time I get paid to move money into my individual brokerage account for investing. Typically, investing at least 10 percent of your salary is a helpful guideline to start building your investment portfolio. It's a percentage that is manageable for many people, but remember, it's not a one-size-fits-all approach. If you can afford to invest more than 10 percent, that's great! The important thing is to get into the habit of saving and investing regularly.

Whether you're a business owner or investing for yourself, another recommendation is to prioritize paying yourself first by setting aside money for investments before spending on other things. This approach will help you spot any potential financial issues early on, including earning or spending problems. Business owners do this by adopting a "profit first" approach to ensure they're allocating profits before expenses and fostering financial stability. You can apply this same method in your own life to help you stay proactive about your financial goals. Another way you can look after yourself is by taking care of your health. You've probably heard the expression "health is wealth," and it couldn't be more true, because if you don't prioritize nurturing your health, you may end up paying the price in medical bills down the road.

In her book *The Top Five Regrets of the Dying*, author Bronnie Ware highlights that three out of the top five regrets relate to finance (specifically, working too hard), relationships (wishing they'd stayed in better touch with their friends), and happiness (wishing they'd done more of what brings them joy). You're probably thinking that I said money doesn't buy happiness.[1] I did, and I stand by that. But money can afford you opportunities to make a difference.

Exercise Your Knowledge

When we practice giving our money, time, and talent to help others, the goal is to be able to give without the expectation of receiving something else in exchange. However, there is a lot we can receive by giving without expecting reciprocity. For example, volunteering can be a rewarding way to build new skills, gain new perspectives, and make a positive difference in the world. Giving freely and generously also enables us to reflect on how giving to others makes *us* feel in terms of our own well-being. When we give, we receive opportunities to grow in our personal sense of empathy and compassion for others, and we are also able to lead by example by demonstrating how small acts of kindness can make a big difference in our communities. Write down some of the things you've received by giving to others and take a moment to celebrate your ability to bless the lives of those around you.

PART III

Changing Your Relationships with Money

CHAPTER 13

Money and Relationships

Although the model for the six drivers of financial fitness is designed to give you the best chance at planning, executing, and fulfilling your long- and short-term financial goals, it's important to remember that this model doesn't exist in a vacuum. In fact, events and people outside of your personal journey can and do have a profound influence over your ability to attain true financial fitness. From lifelong friends and colleagues to the person you marry and the children you raise, the relationships you have will affect your relationship with money.

Consider figure 13.1. With *you* in the center, each circle represents a different type of relationship you will most likely develop at some stage in your life. Your spouse or life partner, as well as your children, will typically be the closest to you, with parents, family, and friends being one circle further out, and individuals in your broader social community being the furthest from you.

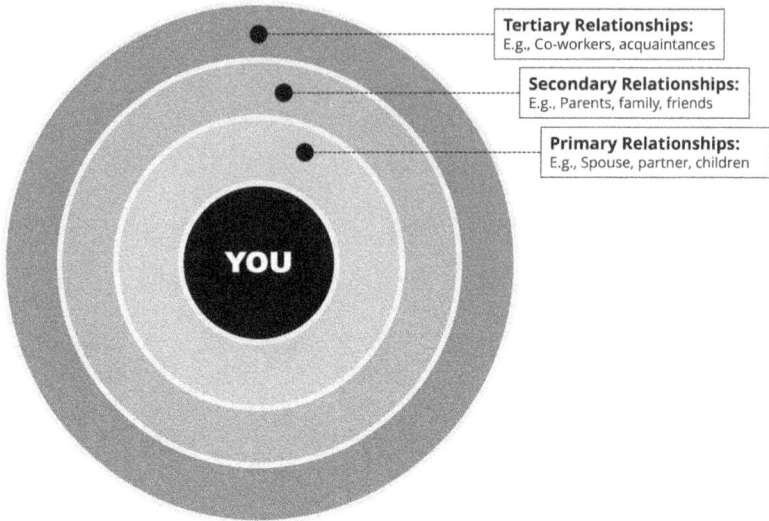

Figure 13.1. The strength and effectiveness of your support system depend on the vast network of interconnected relationships you cultivate, extending from those closest to you to individuals within the outer spheres of your communities.

The closer the circle is to *you*, the more significant those relationships are, and the more significant their impact is on your relationship with money. However, individuals in the outermost circle also can have an impact on your relationship with money. Knowing how to approach each type of relationship appropriately can help you with financial challenges if and when they happen. To help simplify what is otherwise a very nuanced subject, I've broken this chapter into different relationships in the hopes that it will help you avoid some common money problems and address any issues you may struggle with in your relationships.

Money and marriage

Marriage isn't just a union of two people eager to spend the rest of their lives together; it's also a union of their personal financial mindsets. You and your spouse may hold different, or even conflicting, opinions about money—such as how to spend it or when to save it—and that's why taking care of your *collective* financial fitness matters. Whether you're just starting out, have been married for several years, or have been married several times, money can be a stressful subject to talk about with your partner. The sad truth is that roughly one in five marriages will end due to financial stress. The reason talking about money is so taboo is that it highlights where your spouse's priorities lie, which may conflict with what your personal priorities are. Opposing financial ideologies can cause deep emotional and psychological distress in relationships. You've already done some digging and reflecting on what money means to you, your relationship to it, and how it relates to your financial fitness journey. When you commit to a partner, though, getting familiar with what money means to them can make a huge difference when it comes to conflict resolution.

I've alluded to my first marriage throughout the earlier sections of this book, and in particular the emotional and financial impact it had on my life. Since then, finding my true soulmate and marrying my best friend has made my later life a series of incredible adventures. My second marriage is a testament to the power of love, growth, and renewal, and every day I am reminded of how blessed I am to have created such a loving and supportive partnership with someone who is always there to cheer me on. That's not to disrespect my first wife, though.

In my first marriage, we got married very young and (like most couples) had very few assets. As a result, we, like 85 percent of married couples in the United States, opted not to get a prenup, and she moved into my first home. As we embarked on our life together, I came to realize just how different our financial mindsets were, but also how fortuitously they overlapped. For me, money meant having freedom to devote time to my business, have opportunities to travel, and fulfill my role as a leader within my church community. For her, money meant having security, including maintaining a safe, nurturing lifestyle for our kids, which I was willing and able to provide for them.

> **Lightbulb Moment:** Core money values are the building blocks of your financial mindset. Similar to financial scripts, they often develop at an early age. These money values go on to shape how you think about money and have a significant influence on your financial decisions. Keep in mind that core money values can revolve around different beliefs, such as valuing financial security and planning for the future or feeling scarcity and a need to hold on to money tightly. There's no single right way to view your core money values, but when it comes to relationships, being mindful of where yours complement or contradict others' is crucial.

Our core money values start to develop at a young age and, for the most part, are difficult to change. That's why it's crucial to communicate openly and honestly about what your money ideology is right from the get-go. Aligning your financial ideologies starts with getting real about the lifestyle you both want. As individuals, you each have experience with handling your own money, but now you need to figure out how to handle money as a couple. You might agree that one of you should be a stay-at-home parent or that one of you will work part time, or maybe you're both committed to focusing on your careers and working seventy hours a week so you can save as much as possible before you start a family. It's not important what the ideologies are; it's whether they align that matters.

They say that opposites attract, but in my experience, I don't know how much I actually agree with that expression, particularly when it comes to your financial ideology and how similar or different it is from your spouse's. There has been a great deal of research exploring the link between spending habits and personality and how that affects our relationships. Genetic and environmental factors play a role in shaping our personalities, with the five main personality traits being extroversion, agreeableness, openness, conscientiousness, and neuroticism. Sure, everyone needs to spend money on fulfilling basic needs, but how we choose to spend beyond fulfilling those needs is correlated with who we are as individuals. In fact, a huge study investigating over two million bank transactions from citizens of the United States and United Kingdom found that individuals with higher traits of openness spent more money on travel than those who were more conscientious. The same study found that people with more agreeableness traits spent more money on donations, compared to those who were less agreeable.[1] In addition to this, we also have financial personalities shaped by early experiences, social class, and our environment.

Similar to our financial mindset, our financial personality shapes how we think and plan when it comes to money. Types of financial personalities include being a debtor, saver, spender, investor, or giver, and they can mean the difference between paying your bills on time, repeatedly getting hit with late fees, or even planning for and enjoying an early retirement. Like our main personality traits, it's difficult to change financial personalities, but not impossible. By making a conscious effort to work on your financial fitness, you can learn to overcome challenges that come with your financial personality. For example, if you're a spender, you might practice being more self-aware of what you're spending on and evaluate how those purchases correlate with your core values.

Exercise Your Knowledge

One way to level the spending playing field is to practice using the utility cost calculation. Figuring out the cost per use gives both partners a helpful and healthy "measuring stick" to get a sense of the utility or value of a purchase. For example, you might believe that it's better to buy something that costs more because it's higher quality and will last longer, but your spouse may be focused on saving wherever possible and therefore prefers to buy cheaper items. The cost per use of an item may help you evaluate your spending patterns as individuals *and* as a couple. Let's say you're buying a $100 pair of jeans that might last three years. If you wore them every day, that works out to about $0.10 per use ($100/1,000 uses). On the other hand, a cheaper pair of jeans might cost you $40 but only last three months, which works out to $0.45 per use ($40/90 uses), and you'll need to spend another $40 in three months. Think about the last thing you bought (but nothing perishable, like food), then do a quick utility cost calculation based on how long the item lasted or is expected to last. Does the cost per use change how valuable you perceive the item to be?

Now, let's say you're a saver, but you marry someone who is a lifelong spender. When it comes to learning about your partner's financial mindset, it's important to recognize that you and your partner may have come from different backgrounds or may have had different upbringings (remember the ovarian lottery?). Their financial personality will have been shaped by their own experiences growing up, how their parents handled finance, and even the ideologies of the friends in their social circle. In marriages where one partner is more conservative with money, spending can feel intimidating because being financially vulnerable is difficult for them. But beyond clashing personalities, there are a number of things that can cause financial friction in marriages.

Particularly for young couples, the DINK lifestyle (Dual Income, No Kids) can be deceptively alluring. It might initially feel liberating and exciting, but it's easy to under-budget when you're just starting out. A lot of research out there emphasizes that married people live longer, happier lives, but are the benefits the same when it comes to joint finances? Well, yes and no. It's true that dividing cost-of-living expenses makes living more affordable, but when it's two people with two questionable credit histories or two people with large amounts of debt, this can put strain on the financial health of even the happiest couple.

While different spending patterns may cause disagreements, earning differences can also be a source of financial friction. In dual-income marriages where one partner makes significantly less than the other, couples can run into a power struggle when it comes to money. Plus, only about half of all marriages in North America consist of two partners working (though that figure continues to climb). This means that for the other 50 percent of marriages, the responsibility for household income falls on one individual. Even with frequent communication, subconsciously money equates to power, so it may feel like one person has more control over household decisions. A stay-at-home partner may feel insecure about the value they add to the marriage or feel guilty about what they bring to the table. This imbalance can lead to anxiety and resentment in both partners and ultimately leave a couple feeling disconnected.

It's important to remember that just because one person brings in less (or no) money, it doesn't mean they're less important. A partner who stays at home, runs errands, does chores, prepares meals, and helps with homework is essentially doing a full-time job, putting in overtime and extra hours and even working every weekend. And they're *not* getting paid for it—not even minimum wage! I'm not saying you should pay your spouse a salary if they stay at home; however, if you are the higher-earning partner, you should always have gratitude for the person your spouse is and the value they add to your life. Whether the partner who brings in less money works part time or full time to ensure the household is running smoothly, making sure they know how valuable they are in the relationship is crucial. Marriage is about teamwork, and even if you're playing separate positions, what matters is how well you work together.

Having said that, it's nearly impossible to avoid financial arguments altogether, so it's important to have a strategy to address these issues quickly and effectively. When they do happen, try to focus on your own feelings and values rather than trying to explain to your partner what their issue is or why they are the cause of the "problem." Couples who have unresolved financial issues tend to have more frequent and more intense arguments about money, which can ultimately destroy a relationship down the road. That's why being upfront, proactive, and honest about finances will benefit both partners in the long run.

At the end of the day, whether your partner works eighty hours a week and you stay at home or you both work full time and divide the household tasks evenly, whatever you agree on should be what works for you together. To do that, start with aligning your ideologies and expectations. Remember, even if the amount of money you and your partner bring in isn't the same, the value you each give to the relationship will always be equal.

Interestingly, while marriage rates have steadily declined since the start of the twenty-first century, divorce rates have also dwindled in recent years. However, studies continue to show that the more often you get married, the higher your chances are of getting divorced (again). For example, while 53 percent of first marriages end in divorce, that figure increases to 73 percent for third marriages.[2] If you are in your second or third marriage, being transparent about any alimony or child support as early as possible can improve your chances of having a successful marriage.

When it comes to relationships, chemistry isn't an exact science. There's no secret formula you can use to fix any and every problem you run into, because having a stable, loving partnership takes care, hard work, and, yes, compromise. There are, however, key financial milestones that every marriage will go through, and how you (collectively) handle them can actually predict whether the marriage will continue or terminate. You've probably heard the expression "the seven-year itch," which is roughly the length of the average first marriage that ends in divorce. But researchers investigating the psychology behind marriage have also identified a one-year itch and a fifteen-year itch. What's going on during these specific years? As you might expect, marriage milestones play a pivotal role in divorce rates.

In the early years of marriage, most couples are buying their first house, getting their first mortgage, and embarking on a journey to build the life they've both wanted. Everything is new and exciting, but a huge financial obligation like getting a mortgage can cause immediate fractures in the foundation of a new marriage. Around year seven is when couples start talking about having kids and starting a family, which might surface unexpected feelings or conflicting desires that haven't been fully realized or discussed. Misaligned expectations over whether one partner should stay at home versus having both parents work while raising young kids can put strain on the relationship, which might explain why most divorces happen around seven years of marriage.

If couples can work through these itches together, divorce rates do plateau around fifteen years of marriage. By this point, couples have been through a lot of significant changes (both good and bad), they're usually settling into their careers, their children are getting more independent, and they have more experience with handling conflicts in their relationship. In addition, after fifteen years of marriage, couples are more realistic with their expectations than when they're just starting out, which can improve the quality of their relationship with their spouse. However, it is possible for couples to experience that fifteen-year itch I mentioned earlier. One of the main reasons for this is ongoing financial strain, particularly in the form of debt accumulation. That's why it's important to maintain communication and discuss whether you're on track with your mutual financial goals and where you can improve.

Here's the bottom line: Failing to plan for your finances together will ultimately lead to you failing financially. Going through those key milestones without discussing expectations or concerns won't help you avoid unpleasant outcomes. I'm not saying money is the solution to all marital problems—speaking from experience, I know that's not true. You can have more money than you know what to do with and still end up divorced. One study collected data on more than 4,500 couples and found that regardless of debt, income, and net worth, arguments about money were the biggest red flags for divorce.[3] Studies like this remind us that communication is paramount when it comes to finances and relationships. Don't see financial stress as a bad omen; instead, try to embrace it as an opportunity to work together to reach a conclusion that honors your individual and collective values.

✓ **CHECK YOURSELF**

Financial red flags can be a call for couples to act and to change their collective financial mindset. Here are some challenging financial behaviors that you might need to work on in your marriage:

- Not talking about your budget or not knowing where your money is going
- Not spending and saving in accordance with your mutual or collective goals
- Having unrealistic or incompatible expectations
- Being at different places in your financial fitness journey

Someone once told me that marriage is like betting someone half of your stuff that you're going to love them forever. On its face, it's a risky bet, and a costly one if you end up having to pay out. Unlike gambling, though, when it comes to marriage, we can modify the outcomes through our behavior.

We've talked a lot about how financial strain can ruin relationships, but there are many ways we can improve our relationships *without* having more money. It may surprise you, but the number one cited cause of divorce isn't incompatibility, or even infidelity— it's a lack of commitment. Let that sink in. It's a little paradoxical, but the takeaway message is this: Being financially unfit can contribute to greater feelings of detachment, but simply being more financially fit won't prevent an emotionally disconnected couple from getting divorced. Another way of saying this is that a couple is more likely to get divorced due to a perceived lack of commitment than due to financial hardships.

At the end of the day, taking care of our financial fitness is only one component of money and marriage. If we focus on finances and forget to invest in our relationship, we could end up giving half that money away. It's an old cliche, but there's no *I* in team, and at its core, marriage is about teamwork. Think back to what you read in chapter 12 on giving. When you don't dedicate time and energy to making your spouse feel valued and reminding them that they are an equal partner in the marriage, it won't matter how much you earn if you end up giving them half of it and losing your spouse. I do want to be realistic here, though. Big, unexpected things happen in life, and marriages can turn on a dime. You can be on cloud nine with your spouse on Monday and might be in a divorce attorney's office by the end of the week. If you prioritize aligning your ideologies, communicate consistently, and plan for key financial milestones together, chances are you'll have many more happy years of marriage to look forward to.

Money and kids

When it comes to kids, borrowing a phrase from religious leader Dieter F. Uchtdorf, love can also be spelled *t-i-m-e*, and making a conscious effort to spend time nurturing genuine relationships with your kids is just as valuable as making sure you have enough money to provide for them. When we understand the true value of our time, we're more conscious of how we choose to spend it. Giving your time to build strong connections with your kids while they're young can have a lifelong impact on how happy they are and how confident they feel when it comes to being independent in their own life.

Alongside this, I believe that as parents, we have a responsibility to teach our kids about finance and show them how to be financially fit. Realistically, if we don't teach our kids the fundamentals of finance, when they eventually fly the coop and have to make it on their own as adults, they will be dangerously underprepared.

You may be thinking, "Yeah, I definitely want my kids to learn about how to earn, spend, and invest their finances," but across the United States, less than 30 percent of parents are actually talking to their kids about money. For comparison, the number of parents who have talked to their children about sex is around 60 percent (more than double those talking about money!).[4] Interestingly, a large study from Boeing Employees' Credit Union showed that out of a thousand randomly selected adults from a national representative sample, parents reported that they would rather talk about money than sex with their children, but only 28 percent had actually done so. The same study found that fear was a major reason parents avoided discussing money, and three out of four parents believed that they weren't well-equipped enough to teach their children about money. In fact, most parents thought it was best to leave the finance lessons to a professional.[5]

Surprisingly, when researchers questioned young adults about important financial lessons, almost half (44 percent) of Gen Z respondents said that having good spending habits, making and sticking to a budget, and saving for emergencies were the three most important lessons to learn while they were young. If we take a look at more global stats, the number of people who report understanding basic financial topics is just one in three. In countries such as Norway and Denmark, this figure is actually a lot higher (around 70 percent).[6] That's not really surprising, though, because, compared to the United States, countries like these actually implement youth financial education programs that are directly funded by their national banks. What's crucial is that the financial lessons kids learn when they are young influence their attitudes and behaviors when it comes to saving, spending, and investing, and that has a huge ripple effect on the choices they make as adults.

That's probably sufficient for statistics, but the reason I think it's important to include them is to help you understand how your attitudes and beliefs toward teaching kids about money compare with those of other parents. Kids will always be in tune with their household's financial situation even if parents *don't* speak directly about it. What's interesting is that children are more likely to experience financial distress in their own lives if they have witnessed a parent going through a similar hardship.

It's not just about exposure, though; cognitive and personality factors (think financial mindset and financial personality) are also learned through family pathways. Interestingly, genetics account for roughly 50 percent of the difference in financial distress.[7] In 2017, researcher Yilan Xu and their colleagues conducted a study using a sample from the National Longitudinal Study of Adolescent to Adult Health to assess the environmental, cognitive, and genetic factors that can predict financial distress. The study found that genetics played more of a role in determining financial distress at extreme socioeconomic levels (i.e., very wealthy and very poor individuals), with the distress being influenced specifically by traits of neuroticism and cognitive ability.[8]

When I was a kid, money scarcity wasn't something my mom really spoke about often, but even at seven and eight years old, I recognized that times were tough financially. In retrospect, I'd say knowing this unspoken truth heavily shaped the way I thought about money from a young age. Growing up, I was observant and had an inquisitive mind, and I learned from watching my mom divide up her paycheck into a series of envelopes: one for groceries, one for rent, one for utilities, and so on. I would watch how she made the little money she did have stretch far enough to cover all these expenses. She didn't teach me anything about finance or how to calculate intrinsic value, but at the end of the day, that's where I learned about the fundamental principles of sacrifice, hard work, and how to be a good financial steward of my money. From there—learning how to be financially fit—I was able to give myself the confidence to teach others about money, including my own kids.

When it comes to teaching my kids about money, I often have to remind myself just how different money is now compared to when I was a kid. When I was young, money was a tangible thing. I could hold it in my hands, put it in a piggy bank, and see my money grow (literally) as I saved more. I was in charge of every dollar. I could *lose* it, and I knew that that's what made it so valuable. Fast-forward about thirty years, and now the amount of time my kids spend handling physical money is miniscule. It's difficult to teach kids how to be responsible and realistic with money when it's become such an abstract concept. We touched on the downside of digital currency in chapter 10, but when it comes to teaching kids how to be financially fit, using an intangible concept is tricky.

It's bizarre that kids learn about numeracy (i.e., how to work with numbers) when they're around four years old, but they learn about transactions and how to make online purchases before they have any real knowledge of how money works, or that it even exists! When I was a kid, the only money I spent while playing games was for imitation transactions I made in Monopoly. Today, for the majority of children under age five, their only experience with money is through buying power-ups or making in-app purchases. And while this can lead to unintentional spending on parents' credit cards, perhaps the more crucial question is this: How does it affect the development of their financial ideologies?

There is no doubt that early exposure to digital transactions affects children's spending habits later in life, but the research is still unclear on how digital money affects the way children perceive and exercise their own power when it comes to finance. What you should be cognizant about, though, is that gamifying finance for children in this way can give them a distorted perception of how transactions work in the real world and lead to a poor understanding of how easily money can be earned and spent. Don't get me wrong, I'm not a technophobe; in fact, I'm grateful for how convenient technology has made life in the modern world, but developments like these underscore how important it is to educate our kids on the value of money at an early age and instill in them healthy financial behaviors.

Giving your kids an allowance is a great way to encourage positive financial behaviors that can set them up to be successful in the real world. No kid is realistically going to sit and listen to you give a talk about money; that's why it's often more effective to let them experience it for themselves. Giving them the tools to learn how to earn, save, and spend money *before* they get into the real world will give them the confidence and competence to handle their finances in future.

With seven kids, my mom couldn't afford to give us all an allowance, but I made my own pocket money by mowing lawns, shoveling snow, and doing whatever odd jobs I could find. Now that I have kids, my current wife and I have made an effort to teach them about money in a safe, tangible way. In our house, it works like this: My kids get a weekly allowance for keeping their rooms tidy and doing chores around the house. Instead of handing out real money, though, my wife and I give them paper money, which acts as a token IOU they can exchange for real money when they want to make a purchase.

Giving them pretend money to hold on to gives them a sense of financial responsibility without the risk of them misplacing it. When they find something they want to buy, they have to go through the steps of getting their IOUs, counting out the equivalent number of dollars, and giving the fake money over to me or my wife. If they don't have enough to buy the item yet, they have to practice patience or delay gratification until they have saved up enough. The tangible experience of saving physical money, feeling it in their hands, and realizing that they will have less money in their savings jar after they make a purchase forces them to slow down and think about where the money is going.

> **Lightbulb Moment:** Giving kids the freedom to choose how to spend their allowance teaches them about big concepts in a straightforward way. For example, opportunity cost describes the potential benefit we are giving up when we choose one thing over another. In other words, when choosing between two things, the value of the item we don't choose is "lost" simply because we didn't choose it. When asked to choose between two toys, kids will choose the one they value more (adults do this too), but they may not realize what they're giving up by not choosing the alternative.

Talking to your kids about their strategy for saving and spending while they're young is pivotal to their future financial fitness, but I've realized that tact matters when it comes to getting the message across. What they choose to spend their money on may not seem like a valuable purchase to you, but try not to pass judgment on their choices. Avoid saying things like "That's a foolish thing to spend money on" (even if you think it is). Perhaps they chose to spend thirty dollars of their allowance on a toy. Now, imagine if that toy breaks after they play with it just five times. We know from the utility cost example earlier in this chapter that that's a six-dollar-per-use cost, which seems incredibly high. While a child may not understand how to calculate utility costs, they will learn the fundamentals of the same lesson at a much younger age.

And in doing that, they will also have a better understanding of the value of the things they buy and the opportunity cost of choosing to buy one thing instead of another.

I don't necessarily think this strategy works for every parent, but in my experience, it means I never have to feel bad for saying no when my kids want to buy something *and* I know they're learning a valuable lesson about independence when it comes to finance. Unlike when I was a kid, the opportunity for kids to make money nowadays is right at their fingertips. From sponsored social media accounts and YouTube channels, to getting paid to stream themselves playing video games, to selling handmade crafts online, to freelancing, there are infinite opportunities for kids today to earn money. As parents, we should be encouraging them to seek out these opportunities, while making sure they choose legitimate, safe, and responsible ways to make money. In addition, we should teach them important skills for being fiscally responsible with that money.

Money and parents

We've covered the importance of teaching kids to be financially independent, but what about when parents are financially reliant on their kids? It's not uncommon for adult children to feel morally obligated to provide for their parents once they are no longer able to work or they aren't financially secure. And while it can feel good to provide financial support to parents or caregivers as a token of our appreciation, you must make sure that what you're willing and able to provide won't negatively affect your own financial security. Covering the cost of expenses like housing, care, and medication may become a reality for you once your parents reach that age, and that's a part of your financial planning that you can and should be proactive about. That might mean making sure you discuss these potential expenses with your spouse and talking about how these costs affect your own family's immediate and long-term financial goals. Realistically, you are going to outlive your parents, so making sure you've got your own financial house in order before taking on additional financial obligations is crucial. In North America, the number of parents who still financially support their adult children exceeds the number of children who are supporting their parents, but if we look more closely, there are racial and cultural nuances we cannot overlook.

Cultural expectations, religion, tradition, and values all play a role in shaping how people care for their elderly. For comparison's sake, roughly 80 percent of nursing home residents in the United States are White, while just over 5 percent are Hispanic or Latino. In countries like China, as many as 75 percent of elderly people live with or in the same neighborhood as their adult children. Even within the United States, one in four Asian, Black, and Latino households are multi-generational (i.e., adult children live with both their parents *and* their own kids), compared to just 13 percent for White households.[9]

I'm not saying one method is superior to the other; in fact, there are pros and cons to both, but why *are* they so different? Western society emphasizes independence and promotes self-sufficiency when it comes to its children. In comparison, more collectivist cultures like those in Black, Asian, and Hispanic communities raise their children with the understanding that it's normal to provide for their elders and with the expectation that this duty will be theirs someday. A large study evaluating cross-cultural differences in Chinese, South Asian, and Latin American families living in Canada found that these groups placed greater importance on religious duty and family values when it came to providing care for their parents and grandparents and embracing it as an opportunity to serve God (or some higher power) through these services. Studies like this highlight the importance of giving time to relationships and how fulfilling it can be to repay others through service and acts of kindness rather than through financial gifts.

The bottom line is that it doesn't matter what your cultural background is or where in the world you live. Just as planning for your own future is crucial, if you're planning to financially support your parents once they're no longer able to work or earn a living, it's important to consider how things will play out financially ahead of time. For example, you should consider your current and future financial situation, as well as the potential financial position of your parents. That includes factoring in things like planning for how potential long-term care needs could impact your ability to support your parents *and* how supporting them will impact your own retirement plans.

With regard to taking care of parents, I believe there comes a time in life when the responsibilities or roles of caretaker and provider just flip-flop. Growing up, my mom did the absolute most she could to take care of me and my siblings, but now that we're all much older and have jobs and families of our own, we owe it to her to repay that support. I know not everyone will see it that way, but to me, having enough money to provide for her and make her feel taken care of has always been incredibly important to me, and that's why I made it part of my financial plan.

Money and friends

When it comes to friends and finances, my philosophy is to avoid mixing business and pleasure. It's easy to get yourself stuck between a rock and a hard place when a friend asks to borrow money from you, because if you refuse to help them out, they may get upset and grow to resent you. On the other hand, if you do decide to lend them the money and they don't pay you back, you may start to begrudge *them* for breaking your trust and wind up having to have an uncomfortable confrontation. Neither is really a preferable option, so to protect your own financial well-being as well as your friendships, avoid lending money whenever possible.

If you're in a position where you can lend friends money, remember that they may not view paying it back as a priority, particularly if you're able to lend frequently or have a large surplus of money. And even if it feels like you're relieving them of some financial burden, you need to recognize that what you're actually doing is giving them an obligation to pay back additional debt in the future. If we want to be true financial stewards, we must help other people be fiscally responsible, too, and that includes helping friends avoid the dangers of getting into unnecessary debt.

Similarly, we have an obligation to ourselves to not let people or friends outside of our circle negatively affect our own financial fitness. It's understandable that friendships are easily formed among people who can afford to do similar activities, and so people with similar income levels will tend to socialize together more. On the other hand, if we allow money to determine how we spend our time (and with whom), we can end up alienating ourselves and others if we aren't honest about our financial boundaries.

Whether you're saving for a vacation or just need to tighten your budget this month to cover your mortgage, it can feel uncomfortable to decline an invitation from a friend. Just as your spouse's financial ideology may differ from yours, your friends may have different perceptions of wealth and finances. Over time, you may even grow to develop financial mindsets that are surprisingly dissimilar.

I had a great friend in high school—we grew up together, we'd hang out during the summer, and (once we were old enough) we'd go for a few drinks every weekend. As we've gotten older, our lifestyles have changed. We made different career choices, and we're in very different financial situations now, but despite all this, we're still great friends who make a point to keep in touch.

On the other hand, you may lose friendships with people who don't share the same values as you, or you might feel disconnected from those whose financial personalities clash with your own. If I think back to the friends I made in college, I'm more similar to some of the people I'm still close to today than others, but I wouldn't go so far as to say that the reason we *aren't* close is because we're too dissimilar. As we've grown up, made different career choices, and prioritized our personal values, we've built lives that reflect our individual financial mindsets, but it's not our conflicting mindsets that have made it hard to keep in touch; rather, our choices have carried us in different directions.

When we allow ourselves to feel uncomfortable or embarrassed about not being able to afford something in the near term, our ego gets in the way of our relationships. At the same time, if we constantly obsess over trying to impress people with our wealth or try to buy our way into social circles by spending our money on material things, we deprive ourselves of the opportunity to achieve our long-term goals.

✓ CHECK YOURSELF

Similar to lending money to family members or kids, lending money to friends is a lose-lose transaction. When we give someone else money because they don't have the financial capacity to afford something, we aren't just giving away money that we could use in some other positive way, we also are enabling their bad financial habits. It's like the fishing metaphor: Don't just give your friend a fish; teach them how to fish—in other words, teach them to be self-sufficient. Instead of just blindly offering them money, help them learn how to become financially fit on their own (or better yet, give them a copy of this book!). All kidding aside, giving someone the opportunity to understand money is way more valuable than lending it to them. Whether it's for a sibling, a parent, or even your closest friend, remember, a dollar lent is a dollar lost.

Saying no to lending people money might feel uncomfortable, but at the end of the day, it's impossible to have genuine relationships with people if there is an obligation for one individual to lend money to the other. It's that simple. It can be hard to say no to someone you love, but it gets easier with practice. If that sounds harsh, think of this way: If you don't make your mind up ahead of time, eventually you'll find yourself in a situation that requires you to answer someone on the spot. It'll be much harder to say no if you have to think about where you stand on lending money in that moment, but if you stick to your decision early on and make it a rule you live by, you won't be caught off guard down the road.

My personal rule is to never lend people money—not my parents, siblings, or friends. It used to be difficult for me to say no, but when it comes to giving money to people, having boundaries in place can prevent unpleasant fallouts with those you care about. If you are worried about feeling guilty for saying no, remember that if you allow people to depend on you, you are actually limiting their ability to become financially independent. Even if you're just trying to do something positive for them in the short term, lending money to people who have no means or obligation to pay it back actually enables them to continue being financially weak.

Let me give you a personal example. About ten years before he died, my dad called me out of the blue to ask if I could lend him some money. It wasn't a huge amount, and I certainly could afford it at the time, but to be honest, he'd never been willing to provide financially for me or my siblings, so I didn't think I owed him the favor. More than that, though, by that time in my life I had made a vow to myself to never lend anyone any money. I'd lent people money in the past only to have those relationships ruined because things got so uncomfortable when they weren't able to pay me back. So I stuck to my rule and told my dad I couldn't lend him the money. Needless to say, he wasn't very pleased, and that was the last time I ever spoke to him while he was alive. I'm not sharing this to fish for sympathy, but there's a valuable lesson in that story: learning how to say no when people ask you to lend them money. Remember, you aren't responsible for how people respond when you don't give them the answer they're looking for, even if you say no outright. The bigger thing to keep in mind is that if someone is willing to break off their relationship with you because you said no to lending (or giving) them money, that says more about their character than it does about you.

Money matters, cash conflicts, and financial feuds (whatever you want to call them) are very common, and knowing how to handle them in stride is something 40 percent of the US population is still trying to figure out. When it comes to marriage, kids, and friends, money can make or break relationships, but by honoring your financial ideologies and being proactive about planning for financial responsibilities, you can protect your relationships *and* your finances. At the end of the day, I believe the people in our close circles should be there to enjoy the relationship they have with the person we are, not the money we have. If you are adamant about lending someone money, you're better off considering it as a gift rather than treating it as a loan. And if you're in a position to be generous in your life, I hope this next chapter will encourage you to practice being generous with your time rather than your money.

🧠 Exercise Your Knowledge

Reflect back to the beginning of this chapter when we explored the concept of financial relationship circles. Keep this concept in mind as you do this exercise of identifying your inner circle. You might feel vulnerable or as though you're being judgmental in doing this exercise, but the aim here is to better understand who is in your circles, and how your connection to each person impacts you financially.

1. *Identify your inner circle.* List the individuals who have the most significant influence on your finances, such as your spouse, immediate family members, and close friends.

2. *Assess financial impact.* For each person in your inner circle, determine how their financial habits, values, and support affect your own financial decisions and well-being.

3. *Consider your support system.* Evaluate how your inner circle supports you in financial matters. Are they supportive and understanding or do you encounter financial conflicts?

4. *Reflect on your own impact.* Think about how your financial behaviors and decisions might be influencing the people within your inner circle.

5. *Identify areas for improvement.* Are there any relationships that might benefit from better financial communication or collaborative financial planning?

Remember, recognizing areas for improvement in your financial communication within your inner circle isn't a bad thing. In fact, it can lead to stronger, more supportive relationships that support your financial success.

CHAPTER 14

Making Other People Feel Valued

Lightbulb Moment: It costs nothing to be kind to people, but the value of acting with kindness toward others is immeasurable.

Being a positive influence in other people's lives is more than just seeing the glass as half full. It's about acting and interacting with the intention to make genuine connections with people. It's about speaking to others with encouragement and in a way that empowers them to embrace their own unique abilities and pursue their own purposes. And it's about approaching the relationships we form with respect and making sure we are behaving in ways that inspire, uplift, and build others up. It doesn't matter whether it's a partner, a friend, or a complete stranger, when we give time to empowering others, what we're actually doing is encouraging them to take action, be proactive, and innovate for themselves.

If you think about it, every interaction we have has the capacity to create a ripple of influence. If we're constantly berating others and putting them down, these negative ripples will foster negative outcomes; however, if we're conscious about acting with kindness, the positive influence of our interactions will be carried forward. How we treat people can have a huge impact on how happy others are in their lives, but it also holds the key to how fulfilled we feel in our own lives.

Sometimes, we can get so wrapped up in the who, what, when, and where of our lives that we forget to focus on the most important part of living: the *why*. Why am I here on this earth? It's a question every single person on this planet will ask themselves at least once, and the beautiful mystery of life is that each of us will have a different answer. For a long time, I was so focused on living this one life to the fullest—determined to experience everything I possibly could and making sure I didn't miss out on anything—that I was unintentionally keeping myself from answering that very question.

There are limitless things that we can find pleasure in doing, but how do we make sure we live a truly fulfilling life? It's possible that the things we find rewarding don't fulfill us, because being happy and being fulfilled aren't actually the same thing. If that blows your mind, Simon Sinek, a brilliant motivational speaker, says it best: "Happiness comes from *what* we do. Fulfillment comes from why we do it."[1] Don't get me wrong, it's important to lead a life that is both happy and fulfilling, but ultimately, happiness, unlike fulfillment, doesn't last forever. Remember, at their core, emotions (like happiness) are fleeting. In fact, scientists have concluded that emotions only really linger for about ninety seconds in our brains, then they either slowly diffuse or are reactivated by new events. On the other hand, fulfillment is a state of being. It's a mindset we can practice in our approach to everything in life: relationships, work, hobbies, spiritual wellness, and, yes, even money.

For years, no matter how happy I felt or how well things were going in my life, I would inevitably find myself circling back to this question: Why am I here? Not with any judgment or negative emotional undertone, though. I was just in the habit of making time to check in with myself about where I was in life and whether I was fulfilling my purpose. Why am I really here—this soul, in this body, in this specific time and place in the cosmos? What am I *supposed* to be doing here? Often I would sit and try to figure out whether there was more I could be doing to get the most out of my time here on earth. One night, I was feeling a little bit lost in my life. I was assured in my faith and had immense gratitude for the people in my life, but I just wasn't sure I was living out my true purpose. As a leader in my church, I've always been mindful of how I can be a good mentor to others and guide them through difficult times, but this time, I was the one who needed reassurance.

I confided in my wife and told her about my struggle and how I had been feeling stuck in life when it came to fulfilling my purpose. I have immeasurable gratitude for my wife. She knows me inside and out, she knows my strengths and my fears, and while I'm a highly competitive, goal-oriented person, she has the incredible ability to hold up a mirror to the things I'm struggling with and encourage me to reflect on what I can learn from them. So, when I was feeling down in the dumps that night, almost effortlessly she turned to me and said, "Steve, maybe you need to stop thinking about what your own purpose is and shift your mindset to try and think about how you can help others find *their* purpose."

It was like a scene from a movie, when the skies clear up and a brilliant light shines down on the protagonist just as they're realizing how to solve their problem. Maybe the answer to the biggest question of all wasn't about fulfilling *my* purpose, but about helping other people to fulfill theirs. Was that really it? Had I solved life's biggest mystery? Perhaps not, but I finally understood the reason I'd never been able to answer the question of *why* for myself before. I had to shift my mindset from "what can the world offer me?" to "what can I offer the world?" But that wasn't just a simple switch I could flip; I needed to reframe my whole mental script. Every thought and feeling I'd had up until this point in my life and every choice I'd made and how I behaved had been geared toward trying to fulfill myself and my purpose. Now, I had to reframe my thoughts, feelings, and behaviors to figure out how to be an agent for good in the lives of others.

Yes, put yourself first

Our true purpose will only be fulfilled when we become a good influence on those around us. It's taken years for me to realize this, but my hope is that by sharing this knowledge with you, you will be able to carry it forward and be an agent for good for the people in your own life. Let me be clear though, being an agent for good doesn't mean taking on the small stuff for others (like housework or chores). It's about helping them realize that they are capable of doing the "big stuff." That includes turning their ambitions into reality, sharing their passion with the world, and doing the one thing that makes them different from everyone else—the thing they might be holding themselves back from doing. Helping people learn how to fulfill their true purpose is what truly fulfills me.

The caveat is that it's unrealistic to assume you can do the big stuff in your own life (start the business, write the book, connect with people, and instill in them the confidence to dig deep and fulfill themselves) if you're focused on fulfilling someone else's priorities. Just like getting our financial house in order before we can give to others, we have an obligation to ensure we're also doing the "small stuff" for ourselves first before we can help others realize their true purpose. Sure, helping your neighbor rake their leaves or shovel their driveway will make you feel happy (temporarily), but in reality, if they are able to do it for themselves, you shouldn't feel obliged to help them out.

If that sounds selfish, consider this: Being less selfish starts with putting yourself first. You read that right. It sounds backward, but when we take time away from our true purpose to help others with the small stuff, we are burying our true purpose under the obligation to help others. What is truly selfish is not giving ourselves time to figure out how to achieve our own big stuff, the things that will have a monumental impact on our ability to touch the lives of others. Simply being philanthropic is a great way to do good in the world, but aligning our thoughts, feelings, and behaviors so we can pursue our true purpose is the only sure way of leaving something meaningful behind once we're gone.

Often, we assume that selfishness simply means refusing to help others, but in reality, if we spread ourselves too thin because we're constantly trying to do the small things for everyone else, we can hinder our ability to do the big stuff. We can make more of an impact by focusing on big-picture influence through building up others and strengthening their belief in themselves so they feel not just capable, but also destined and motivated to do the big picture things for themselves.

On the other hand, being a positive influence means working on your relationship with yourself. You cannot lift others up to be the best, most successful, or most fulfilled version of themselves if you aren't leading by example. That doesn't mean you have to be perfectly fulfilled before you start making others feel valued, but it's essential to continue building yourself up in order to continue helping others do the same. For me, being an influence for good meant I had to focus on learning new skills, overcoming hardship, improving my financial literacy, and figuring out how to align my daily patterns with my goals. Doing that allowed me to open myself up to being a mentor for others, teaching them how to align their thoughts, feelings, and behaviors so they could go out into the world and be an agent of good.

So, being selfish in some ways can help you to help others, but it doesn't mean making yourself the center of the universe. If the aim of fulfillment is to be a good influence on people, it requires us to give others the conviction that they are also valuable here on earth. Going back to having gratitude for our place in life, we have to remember that we aren't alone here. Beyond the people we hold in our circles—our spouse, kids, parents, siblings, and friends that play a part in our story—there is a whole world out there filled with people who have their own stories. While we won't connect with each and every one of them, we can make an effort to connect with those with whom we do cross paths. One simple way to connect with people is to ask them, "Hey, how's your day going?"

On a side note, asking people open-ended questions like this can have a pretty profound effect on us. While doing some research for this chapter, I came across an article about a concept called neuroplasticity, which essentially describes the brain's ability to adapt and rewire new cell networks. The article explained that asking questions (particularly insightful ones) causes the brain to release serotonin, which puts our entire brain into a state of reflection and allows us to relax. Once that happens, we're actually able to gather information from all areas of the brain at once, which helps to strengthen new neural connections that can get us a little closer to finding a solution to our own problems. It sounds like science fiction, but it's a legitimate technique you can use next time you're stuck on a problem.

The importance of connecting

Connecting with others isn't just about flexing our brain muscles, though; it's about being genuinely interested in how people arrived at where they're at in life. People are *fascinating*, and the odds are that anyone will fascinate you in some way or another if you give them the chance. A huge part of embracing an abundance mindset is learning to resist the urge to talk about ourselves all the time. Yes, many of us could fill a whole library with stories from our own life, and yes, many of us are passionate about teaching others what we know. But one of the most rewarding lessons we can learn is to give someone else the space and time to share their story. Remember, you *matter*, and so does everybody else. So, when it comes to the archive of stories about yourself that you're holding on to, make sure you've got space somewhere on the shelf for someone else's story too.

In his book *The Gift of Influence*, Tommy Spaulding talks about how, over the course of our lifetime, we will influence around eighty thousand people—enough to fill a whole football stadium. Some of them will be people we interact with on a daily basis, but others won't even remember our name. Those who know us personally will remember the details of the things we did in our life, and those who don't will only remember how our words and actions made them feel. The takeaway message is this: However brief, we have the capacity to influence the lives of others (positively or negatively) simply by interacting with them.

You don't have to ask every person you meet to tell you their entire life story, but don't just ignorantly shuffle through life either. Pay attention to the people around you and take an interest in who they are. If they're dressed really sharply, give them a compliment; if you can see how hard they're working, acknowledge it. If you notice something about someone that holds your attention long enough for you to make a positive judgment about them, just say it out loud, no strings attached! Given the nature of my work, I'd probably bet I will interact with more than a stadium's worth of people over my lifetime. I don't think that makes me a more important person, but it's taught me a critical lesson that I want to share with you: Opportunities come from people, *not* things.

It's my personal philosophy that everything happens by divine design. I don't believe in coincidences because I know that every single person I encounter in my life will nudge me in the direction I need to go, and the connections I make will bring me the opportunities I need. Now, does that mean I don't have any influence over which direction my life goes? Of course not. It's still up to me to connect with people and be open to learning what they can teach me through our interactions, but when I make sure I approach every interaction with the desire to build others up or make people feel valued, then whatever ripples I create from my interactions will have a positive influence.

The exciting part is that the more positive ripples you create, the more likely you are to feel the effects of those interactions. When that happens, you can be sure that when you encounter the effects of these positive interactions, they are moving you toward other good outcomes and the path of fulfillment. I'm not talking abstractly here in terms of "where I'm going"; in fact, I'm being quite literal. The connections we make with people can put us on unexpected trajectories that take us to incredible places in life.

It's astounding, but when I truly think about it, every job I've ever done in my life (even going back to my summer sprinkler gig) I got because I *connected* with someone. Having a degree, which is essentially a small, very expensive piece of paper, can never do what authentic human connection can. For example, when I was in college, I got placed with a guy from one of my business class projects. His name was Sam, and we sort of hit it off. We graduated and went our separate ways, and then, seven years later, we reconnected completely out of the blue. As it turned out, Sam knew the CEO of a big pharmaceutical technology company in California who was looking for a CFO, and lo and behold, he'd recommended *me*. Not because of my degree, but because we'd made a lasting connection all those years ago. Giving time to that connection brought the opportunity to me. In the end, I didn't end up taking that job offer, but the moral of this story is that the more we engage with people with that mindset of abundance and with the intention to create as many ripples of positive influence as we can, the more new connections we'll create for ourselves, and the more open we'll be to embracing the new opportunities that come with them.

✓ CHECK YOURSELF

If the thought of complimenting a complete stranger, or striking up a conversation with someone you frequently see on your commute, or just trying to connect with people around you on a deeper level makes you nervous, ask yourself: What's the worst that could happen? Remember the pyramid example in chapter 4, where the worst possible outcome is usually the most unlikely? When it comes to taking risks to make connections with people, the worst that's going to happen is that your life is going to be exactly the same. Perhaps you'll feel a little embarrassed for a few minutes if the recipient doesn't share in your enthusiasm to connect, but in the grand scheme of things, your life will carry on as normal . . . not so scary, right? On the other hand, it's possible that taking that risk could lead to a connection that changes your life forever. The choice is yours—will you choose predictability or possibility?

"How did I do?"

When you're actively connecting with people, keep in mind what it is that people actually *want*. It's a vague premise, but one of the universal truths about humans is that they desire what they value, and they value what they desire. The late psychologist Steven Reiss dedicated his life to studying the motivations behind human desire. While doing a large cross-cultural study, he identified sixteen basic human needs, ranging from power to tranquility, romance to vengeance, and everything in between. According to Reiss, all of these emotions are deeply rooted in human nature and are reflected in the way we think, feel, and behave, but the way we prioritize these desires is unique to each of us. (Sound familiar? It should!)

At a much more primal level, though, humans crave the assurance that they belong and that they *matter*. Genuine connectedness starts with showing people they are valued. When we feel disconnected, we're more likely to experience anger, anxiety, depression, jealousy, and sadness, and we're less likely to pursue new connections. People want to be seen and heard, and it's up to us to make that happen. We should always lead with respect; this lets them know they are understood and validated. It gives them a sense of value, which ultimately assures them that they matter. Regardless of how we prioritize our other desires, this is the one universal desire we humans share. Oprah Winfrey noted that throughout her career, no matter the background of her guests, every single interview she gave ended with the person asking the same question: "How did I do?" It didn't matter whether she was speaking to a president, a world-class athlete, or even a man who was in jail for murdering his twin daughters; every person wanted to know how they did. She soon realized this question wasn't actually about whether the interview had gone well or poorly, but rather, it was their way of asking, "Did I say anything that mattered?" I guarantee you, every person on this planet wants to feel that they're significant.

They want to know that they're important and that they add value to the world, not necessarily through the things they do but simply because of who they are. When we start listening to people with the intention of validating what they're saying, we're able to connect with them on a much deeper level.

Exercise Your Knowledge

Authenticity is hard to fake, and if you try to fake it, it can actually have the opposite effect on people. Here are some tips on how you can foster genuine connection with the people you meet that might lead to unexpected growth in your own life:

- Unclench. If your body is stiff, the conversation will be too.
- Be honest about who you are. Don't lie to try and impress people.
- Be present. Appreciate your capacity to learn from what others have to say.
- Listen. Listen to understand and to validate rather than just respond.

Focusing on others

Helping others find their true purpose starts with taking a genuine interest in their lives. I had to learn to shift the focus in my life from myself to everyone else around me. It's easy to get wrapped up in the narrative of our own lives, but if we want to truly be a positive influence on others, we must make an effort to understand what their story is, learn what they're struggling with, and identify how we can be an agent for good in their life.

I remember quite clearly the moment I realized just how seldom I focused on others. It was in 2019, during a period when I was spending a lot of time giving presentations and keynote addresses, and I was desperate to learn more about how to write and deliver a compelling speech. I attended a communication skills and leadership coaching seminar with a company called Duarte (founded by a woman I highly respect, Nancy Duarte). During the first lecture of the seminar, the speaker pulled up his first slide, which had only three words on it: "Start with empathy." *Boom*. It seemed so glaringly obvious that I actually felt a little embarrassed I hadn't realized it sooner. For so many years, I'd gone into my presentations with all the enthusiasm to talk about what I thought was interesting, but without a second thought about what the audience might want or need to hear. My whole focus had been on myself rather than on others—on talking about what mattered to me rather than listening to what mattered to others.

Just as I had learned to shift my mindset from pursuing my own fulfillment to helping others fulfill themselves, I now had to learn to shift my focus from simply teaching others to listening and understanding what they truly needed. Up until that point, I'd been so focused on the grind that I would block out entire weeks of my life on my calendar. I'd find myself hurrying people to say or do what they had to as quickly as possible, because I was always focused on the next thing I had to do—on what was coming *next*. I realized that focusing on the grind alone wasn't going to give me that truly abundant life I was chasing. Instead, I needed to invest time in making connections and helping other people feel valued and heard, because without relationship abundance, our financial abundance won't be very valuable at all.

Lightbulb Moment: I've said this before, but it bears repeating: The most valuable thing you can give someone is your time. Regardless of wealth, the most successful people are those who give their time to others. When you approach people with a perspective of empathy and use compassion as a tool to be an agent for good in the lives of others, genuine connection becomes effortless.

I've learned so much more about what fulfills me by helping others realize their purpose than I did when I was focused on myself. If you want to make connections with people, practice listening with the intention to understand what they really need and then help them figure out how to get there.

Remember, everybody is on a different page in their story, and a huge part of helping others overcome struggle is understanding the difference between giving counsel and giving advice. To clarify, giving counsel can involve asking the person questions and helping them reframe their problems to find solutions based on what's best for them. Giving advice is simply offering people recommendations based on what has personally worked for you in the past. Now, here's the zinger: When it comes to resolving an issue, we are more receptive to receiving counsel, but people are generally more geared toward giving advice. So why is counsel more effective? Well, I believe that it's because advice can be given anywhere and anytime from anyone, but we can only get counsel from those with whom we are connected. When we share a connection with someone who is willing to give us counsel, we are more inclined to open our hearts and our minds to receive it.

The main takeaway here is this: Stop "should-ing" people. Telling people what they *should* be doing won't actually help them with their problems. It might feel like you're being helpful, but telling them to do what has worked for you might not be a realistic solution for them. Instead, meet that person where they're at. Helping them learn how to reframe their specific problems and identify strategies to overcome what they're struggling with will be more effective than just offering them advice based on what you think is best for them. I'm *not* saying we should never offer solutions; I'm simply demonstrating that it's important to tailor our solutions to the needs of the individual. This strategy doesn't just work for making connections with people, though—it works for all types of relationships you might come across. For example, if you're chasing a job in a specific field, before you go in for your interview, spend some time looking into what the field is lacking. What are the core challenges facing the industry you want to go into? Instead of making it about what the job can do for you, meet the company where they're at, show them that you understand what it is they *need*, and then talk about how you can offer strategies to help solve those issues.

Helping people feel valued

Learning to be a positive influence on people's lives so you can encourage them to find their true purpose isn't difficult, but there are several things you can do to get yourself into the mindset of making others feel valued. First and foremost, lead by example. Listen with the intention of making people feel heard and understood. Second, learn to recognize the type of support people need. Often, support just means encouraging someone to pursue their ambitions or offering them guidance on how to get there. Sometimes, though, people might require resources beyond your support, including things like time or money. If that's the case, remember to only give within your means, and if you do give money, consider it a gift rather than a loan. Finally, positive language goes a long way in terms of building people up. Give them hope, encourage them to have faith in themselves, and remind them of their own capacity to generate ripples of positive influence on the world. By being a positive influence in people's lives, you can encourage them to grow and develop, reach their full potential, and make a positive impact on the world around them.

One of the most remarkable things I've learned in shifting my focus from how I can fulfill myself to how I can influence others is just how incredible our capacity for making connections is. Feeling connected and accepted comes from a social perspective, but the weird and wonderful truth is that these connections actually stem from a biological phenomenon known as mirroring. Get this: We actually have a collection of neurons (a.k.a. brain cells) dedicated exclusively to making connections with other people. How amazing is that? With mirroring, we mimic the behavior, facial expression, and emotional tone of the person we're interacting with. In this way, we are able to show people that we have empathy for them and understand their feelings and struggles, without even saying a word. It's like mind control . . . sort of.

For the most part, this happens subconsciously, but we can also mirror people without interacting with them in person. For example, you can mirror the behavior of people you admire, learn what habits they follow that make them so successful, and mimic them in your own life to manifest that same success. Mirroring is the force that attracts similar things together; whether that's a friend, a colleague, or a client, similar people will gravitate toward one another. If you're someone who exudes positivity, odds are that you'll attract like-minded people in your life.

Unfortunately, it works the other way around too. If you have a negative outlook on things, you're more likely to befriend similarly sour people. It's so much bigger than that, though, because just by having an attitude of gratitude and a mindset of abundance, you can actually attract even greater, more abstract things in your life such as a job or an entire lifestyle because you're more likely to be receptive to connections and opportunities that will get you there.

Exercise Your Knowledge

Think about a time when someone made you feel truly valued and heard. How did that experience make you feel, and what kind of connection did it create with that person? Reflect on the positive emotions and sense of trust that this interaction might have generated.

Conversely, consider a time when you tried to make someone else feel valued. How did you approach the situation and what impact did your actions have on the relationship? If you haven't had the opportunity to do so yet, imagine how you would approach making someone feel valued using the steps we discussed in the chapter: leading with empathy, listening actively, being open to learning, and using positive language.

By reflecting on these experiences, you can gain a deeper understanding of the power of genuine connection and the positive impact it has on your relationships.

PART IV

Taking Action

CHAPTER 15

The Missing Component of the Laws of Attraction and Vibration

You've probably heard the expression "You reap what you sow," but what does it mean in the context of manifesting a life of abundance? How can we acquire tangible things through a seemingly abstract process? As you may have guessed, the cognitive reframing exercise in chapter 3 comes from one of the principles of the law of attraction, which is the philosophical belief that positive thinking leads to positive outcomes, while negative thoughts attract negative outcomes. If we dig a little deeper, though, the law of attraction actually builds on the scientific principle that every single thing in our universe is constantly vibrating at an invisible energetic frequency.

Lightbulb Moment: You might remember your fifth-grade science teacher explaining to you that atoms are the building blocks of *everything*. Atoms, which are made up of positively and negatively charged energy particles, bond together to form molecules that then form structures that make up things (like you and me!). Here's the exciting part: Each bond vibrates at a certain frequency and in a specific direction, meaning that everything, everywhere, at *all* times is vibrating at just the right speed and frequency to keep the universe running smoothly.

So, where do we fit in? Well, similar to the law of attraction, where like things are drawn to one another, the scientific principle regarding vibrations holds that things that vibrate at similar frequencies attract one another. So, if everything, including us, is made up of vibrating energy, it stands to reason that if we're vibrating positively (theoretically or literally), we'll attract people and things that vibrate at a similar frequency. On its face, this premise makes a lot of sense, but is this law of vibration scientifically sound?

The late Masaru Emoto, a Japanese businessman and pseudoscientist, is perhaps most famously known for his experiment on water molecules and ice crystal formation. Emoto believed that he could influence the formation and quality of ice crystals by exposing two identical glasses of water to either positive or negative words, visuals, and music. After a few days of treating the two glasses of water, he froze both glasses and examined the ice crystals closely under a microscope. What he found was that the water that he'd spoken gently to and exposed to positive stimuli had formed beautifully perfect crystal structures. In comparison, the water that had been mocked and treated "badly" created ice crystals that were fractured and ugly. At the end of his experiment, he concluded that humans, like water, can be influenced by the nature of emotions and vibrations in their own environments.

Now, I wish I could tell you otherwise, but unfortunately there isn't actually any scientific proof to these findings. That doesn't mean things in nature aren't affected by vibrating energy, though. In fact, other studies have asked this same question and gotten surprising results. One 2014 study found that plant leaves can actually distinguish between vibrations caused by an environmental threat (e.g., a hungry caterpillar) and vibrations caused by nonthreatening factors, such as wind.[1] In a series of controlled experiments, these researchers were able to demonstrate that plants not only can tell what type of vibration it is, but they also can make selective responses based on whether the vibration poses a threat. Specifically, they found that the plants exposed to the vibration of a caterpillar munching on its leaves would increase their release of mustard oils, a type of chemical defense. When exposed to nonthreatening vibrations in their environment, the same plants had no defense response at all.

Well, that's a little more promising evidence, but what about us humans? Another study found that people who are in the habit of prolonged negative thinking are more likely to experience difficulty reasoning and forming memories later in life.[2] That's likely because negative thinking promotes energy-draining emotions like anxiety and depression, which can deplete the brain's resources and lead to cognitive complications down the road. Positive thinking, on the other hand, improves feelings of joy and fulfillment that actually encourage the brain to make more neural connections to keep you healthy and happy.

Since humans are inherently social creatures, there is an evolutionary advantage to being able to identify and respond to other vibrations. Typically, we classify the vibrations of people, places, and things as either "good" or "bad" vibes. David R. Hawkins, a psychiatrist, physician, and spiritual teacher, devised an entire scale to distinguish between low- and high-level energy and the emotions associated with each. On his scale of one to a thousand, positive vibrations are thought to be high-frequency thinking patterns, attitudes, and emotions, while negative vibrations come from low-frequency thinking patterns, attitudes, and emotions.[3] So, fear-driven emotions, including superiority, anger, fear, sorrow, and shame, all resonate at low-energy levels (below 200 on the scale), and love-driven emotions, including joy, relaxation, creativity, gratitude, and peace, all vibrate at much higher energy levels (around 800 on the scale). But what do we actually mean when we talk about someone else's "vibe"? In psychological terms, someone's positive or negative energy is a result of their mindset, mental scripts, and experiences that have shaped their beliefs and understanding of the world. Essentially their vibe is similar to their attitude toward life. When we're on the receiving end of someone's energy, we feel it through our interactions with them. Someone who resonates with high-frequency vibrations is likely to make us feel calm and at ease, but someone with a negative vibe might leave us feeling worried, angry, and even unmotivated. In a roundabout way, these abstract concepts have a very real place in determining the life we live.

Work hard

Theories from the laws of attraction and vibration underlie the premise of a number of self-help books like *The Secret*, which ultimately don't change people's lives in the way they promise. The main issue that I (and many other people who didn't *vibe* with the book) have with gimmicks like this is that they're so focused on the power of positive thoughts and how important it is to transform how you think that they overlook where the *true* power lies—how we *behave*. Don't get me wrong, I genuinely believe that what you put out into the world is what you attract in your own life; however, I believe it has nothing to do with wishful thinking and everything to do with how we *act*. You will create the life you hold in your mind, and when you look around you, you'll see exactly what you want to see (or what you tell yourself you should see). If you're a fearful person, the world will seem scary. If you're an angry person and you put that energy out into the world, you'll attract other angry people who will reinforce your beliefs and validate your assumptions. And in doing that, you will create a reality that supports those emotions.

What you can't do is just say to the Universe, "I need a new job," or "I have to get my car fixed," and then expect that, through the power of positive thinking, it's going to happen. That's an incredibly naive, not to mention *unfulfilling*, way to live. It sounds great, but it'd be too easy if it really worked like that. If that were true, anyone could just manifest their way to a giant house, great job, and perfect life without ever having to lift a finger. And while there is a kernel of truth to the laws of attraction and vibration, these constructs are incomplete. They're missing one key component, and that's *hard work*. It seems obvious, so why don't they talk about it? Simple: It's hard to sell someone on the idea that they have to do things for themselves. People want a silver bullet, a quick-fix, get-rich-fast solution. Here's the thing: Having a positive mindset will increase your ability to seek out opportunities that might get you to your end goal, but the only way to really get something done is to do it.

To prove just how adamant I am about this, I took it upon myself to impart some of this knowledge to my kids. I was determined to teach them about the laws of attraction and vibration (and hard work), so we sat down together and decided on a collective goal that we wanted to reach as a family. After much debating, we settled on a pair of electric bikes for the family. At the time, my kids were seven and ten years old, so they weren't able to ride the bikes themselves, but they were only too happy to be able to hop on the back of the bikes while my wife and I did all the legwork. So, despite the fact that they weren't strictly going to be able to *use* the bikes, they wanted to be part of the experience of figuring out how we were going to raise enough money to buy them. To make things interesting, we gave ourselves one golden rule: We couldn't use any money we already had. My kids weren't allowed to donate their pocket money toward the bikes, and I wasn't allowed to pay for the bikes with money from my salary, my consulting business, or anything I had in my savings. I had to get the money some other way, using positive thinking (and a few entrepreneurial tactics). For the cost of both bikes, we needed exactly $3,333.13, and I was determined to get every penny without breaking the rule.

I started out by selling my Peloton, which got me $1,200, and then I urged my kids to look around the house to see what else we could sell. A few weeks went by, and we'd managed to sell some old furniture and a mountain bike, but we were still only halfway to our goal. The kids started getting a little discouraged and impatient, but I was determined to show them that wishing for something isn't enough. This was different than just "manifesting." The four of us were actively seeking opportunities to earn the money we needed. Nobody was coming to us asking to buy our stuff; we were out there making it happen. The kids begged me a few times to just buy the bikes and put the money back into my savings, but I insisted we were going to do things the right way—even if it meant doing things the *long* way.

Then, something unexpected—and a little serendipitous—happened, and this is where it seemed like manifesting was working. Out of the blue, I received a letter saying that I had an outstanding federal tax credit of four hundred dollars. Since it was totally unexpected, I put it into our savings. Then, a few weeks later, I got another notice. This time it was from my health insurance provider, saying they were going to reimburse me for overpaying on a medical bill the year before. Random things like this continued to happen from time to time, and every dollar added up, until a few months later, we had saved more than four thousand dollars. *We did it!* I finally bought the bikes a few weeks before Thanksgiving, and my kids, my wife, and I enjoyed a few e-bike adventures before the winter weather set in.

Sure, I could have bought the bikes right from the beginning so we could enjoy them while the weather was still nice, but where's the fun in that? I was determined to teach my kids that you can have whatever you want in this life and you should have faith in your ability to manifest anything you desire, whether it's starting a business, climbing Mount Everest, or winning a Nobel Prize. *However*, part of that lesson is understanding that, at the end of the day, manifesting means nothing if you're not willing to sacrifice things, delay your gratification, and work hard for it. My hope is that in giving my kids the opportunity to exercise their faith and showing them a tangible example about sacrifice and hard work while they're young, they will carry forward a lesson that is far more valuable than just buying them the bikes.

In the Bible, the parable of the talents teaches us we should not be fearful or scared to act boldly when it comes to the things we want. When we are afraid, we manifest scarcity, but when we are assured in what we want and are willing to act in accordance with our desires, we manifest success. It's important to remember that success does not simply mean money. Money could be a consequence of success, but there are plenty of wealthy people who aren't very successful at all. People can be born wealthy (or into wealthy families), but nobody is born successful.

If this book teaches you anything, let it be this: Success isn't measured by how quickly you achieve your goals; it's about continuing to chase your goals even when things set you back. Because I guarantee you, there will be setbacks. Whether you're chasing something specific like starting your own business or something less concrete like a lifestyle, success is an iterative process that requires hard work and repetition. Someone else might be born into more fortunate circumstances that allow them to walk a path with fewer obstacles, but their fortune doesn't mean you're unable to succeed. I believe that anyone can create the life they want, not simply by manifesting it into existence, but through tenacity, strategy, and consistency.

Tenacity is about learning to thrive wherever you're planted in life. I saw this lesson put into practice during my New Delhi trip when I came across a tree growing among a pile of rocks on the side of a mountain. I was dumbfounded at how well this tree was thriving in such a hostile environment. Back home in the States, my landscaping company was setting up irrigation systems and planting trees in the richest, most fertile soil we could find only to have them die. This tree was determined to grow in the most unlikely place without anyone else looking out for it. Whenever I find myself in a tough spot in life, I think back to that tree and how unapologetically it thrived in its surroundings. If a tree can do that, there's no reason we shouldn't be able to find a way to thrive in any situation.

Having a good strategy is more than half the battle when it comes to being successful. It means making sure you're taking action to get what you want. I've spoken to so many people who love to talk about what they're planning on doing and all the different things they have to get done to achieve their plans, and I've realized that the people who talk the most usually make the least progress. Yes, it's great to share your excitement about your goals with the people around you, but if you come across someone who is more focused on talking rather than on taking action, chances are they'll still be talking about their ambitions in six months' time instead of living out their vision. So, when it comes to getting what you want, be aware of how much you're talking about doing it and how much you're actually doing it. Just like I taught my kids while we were saving up for the e-bikes, talking generates nothing; actions generate results. Regardless of how big or small the end goal is, you will end up getting there as long as you continue taking small, meaningful steps toward it.

Work smart

It doesn't matter how long it takes you—be consistent. There is immense power in small, simple actions. From Mozart to Mark Zuckerberg, every successful person who came before you had to endure trial, embrace error, and overcome countless failures to find their success. I guarantee their first attempt at composing a concerto or writing code was far from the masterpieces they went on to create, but each failure brought them one step closer to success.

In his book *Outliers*, author Malcolm Gladwell talks about the ten thousand-hour rule, which is essentially the number of dedicated, focused hours of practice needed to become an expert in any given field. That's a crazy amount of hours, but that's kind of the point I'm trying to make. Good things take time; great things take a really long time. There are no shortcuts on the path to success. There are detours and roadblocks, and there may be accidents at times, but there are no shortcuts. Your first attempt at something likely won't be perfect, and your second attempt might not be either, but each time you try will get you one step closer to your goal. Here's the caveat, though: If you're focused on simply staying busy and not paying attention to your strategy, it is possible to work tirelessly and still not get to where you want to be. It's important to be intentional with your time and make sure you're working smarter, not harder.

Make no mistake, it's possible to work hard and not get to where you want to be. Part of working smarter is about knowing what's worth sacrificing. Whether it's a plan to run a business, buy a house, or teach your kids a valuable life lesson, I like to think of it like this: For everything you do, there's a good, better, and best option. When we plan, we take the time to consider all possible options so we can determine the best outcome and then develop a strategy to get there. If we don't plan accordingly, we'll burn out trying every possible option until we get to the one we want. Sometimes, sacrifices aren't easy to make, but if we're focused on the most essential thing, the best outcome rather than just a good outcome, our sacrifices feel more worthwhile.

Back when I was working as the CFO out in Chattanooga, one of the company presidents came into my office one day and sat down in the chair across from me in a complete fluster. I could tell from his demeanor that he was giving off some low-frequency vibrations. He explained that he was overwhelmed at work and had been putting in so many hours that he'd hadn't seen his family in weeks. His wife was feeling dejected, and he'd been getting home after his kids went to bed, so he was barely spending any time with them. I could see he was in a vulnerable place, and I understood why he was frustrated.

"Look," I said to him, "this company is losing millions of dollars a year, but there are absolutely no rewards for efforts. Don't confuse efforts for results." With that, I sent him home to have dinner with his family. In my mind, he was focusing all of his energy on the company, which was good, but I could see that what was *best* for him (and his family) was sitting down and reconnecting with his loved ones. There are no rewards for efforts and no participation trophies in life. The takeaway is that if you're focused on just acting, you might end up only achieving what's good rather than what's best. And if you're completely focused on the efforts—or worse, stuck just *talking* about your efforts—you might wind up missing the results you want altogether.

If I'm being honest, I'm a textbook type A person. I'm highly ambitious, goal-oriented, and self-motivated. I've never had to worry about not spending time doing the "good" things, but I've learned over time how to focus more on achieving the "best" stuff. When I left my job in Chattanooga, I decided I was going to take some time off. Fortunately, I was in a financial position to be able to do that, but when I told people that I'd be taking six months off from work, they *laughed.* Out loud. "You can't even take a month off," they said. "In fact, I'd put money on it that you won't last a week."

Well, they were wrong. I didn't even last a day! The very next morning, I was up at 5:00 a.m., took myself for a run, and by 7:00 a.m., I was back in my office working on my next business idea.

That's just one example, and getting things done *does* make me feel amazing, but in retrospect, this might not have been what was best for me. What might have been better or even best for me and my family would have been to take some time off, slow down a bit, and spend time with the kids while I figured out what I wanted to do next. I absolutely love spending time with my kids, and I would genuinely take any opportunity I can to do so, but slowing down is not something I'm particularly good at. Being able to take time off and put work aside for a few days is something I aspire to be able to do, and it's certainly something I've worked on over the years. The thing is, in this day and age, there's so much pressure on staying productive and working hard that stepping away from my professional ambitions can feel intimidating.

If you are ambitious and can identify with parts of my story, that's great, because you're not alone. Just make sure that while you're running around being ambitious, you're working in pursuit of the best possible outcomes and not just rushing to settle for what is good. I'll be the first to admit that I'm not perfect, and at the time it felt like I was doing something great, but this is an excellent example of where I probably could have spent a little more time thinking beyond what was good and instead pursuing what was best.

Energy management

They say that time is money, but when it comes to success, managing your energy is crucial too. From the launch of the World Wide Web to the first successful genetic cloning, the 1990s was a decade of significant developments in the fields of science and technology. As a young businessman, though, the thing I remember most about the nineties was how obsessed everyone was with time management skills. It was a craze that swept across the world as people wanted to learn how to manage their time more efficiently. They were under the assumption that poor time management was standing in the way of their success, and I genuinely thought so too. It made sense that if people weren't managing their time, they wouldn't get the results they wanted. For years, I went around giving presentations and keynote addresses on how to successfully manage time, but with the benefit of hindsight, I know now that's only half the truth. A lot of people I meet with are highly ambitious, results-driven individuals who know how to manage their time well enough, but when it comes to execution, they struggle to find the energy to actually get things done. Imagine a seesaw, with time on one side and energy on the other. Success will only manifest when there is a balance between our energy and our time. We need to find the equilibrium between managing our time and our energy.

Plenty of books claim they can help you manage your time, but how can we manage our energy better? It's actually quite simple: identify what it is that gives us the most energy and then do *more* of it. For example, my morning routine is planned around doing things that energize me. That means waking up early, taking time to move my body, reading Scriptures, and journaling while everyone else in my household is still asleep. I know that won't work for everyone, but if we don't invest time into doing things that energize us, we're guaranteed to get ourselves stuck in a downward spiral of things that deplete us. Not doing what we love is, in some ways, a waste of time. Here's why: Going back to the law of vibration, if you're depleted and exhausted because you aren't spending time doing what you love, you're probably going to be vibrating at those lower frequencies, which will leave you feeling depressed and unmotivated. You could schedule every hour of your entire workweek, and by the end of it, if you haven't made time to replenish your energy, you'll probably feel too depleted to do any of the things you really want to do. And guess what? Not spending time doing what energizes you will negatively impact your motivation and productivity the following week. So, when it comes to managing your time, make sure you leave room in your schedule to dedicate a few minutes to manage your energy too, because without both, you will never be able to create those best outcomes.

✓ CHECK YOURSELF

Doing more of what energizes you can revolutionize how effectively you use your time, but how can you figure out what those things are? If you're feeling stuck, try asking yourself the following questions:

- What am I most passionate about?
- What do I love talking to other people about?

continued

- What event or activity am I looking forward to right now?
- What activities help me "switch off"?
- When I finish doing _ _ _, I feel motivated and empowered to act!

Getting back to business, when it comes to being the creator of your own success, my advice to you is this: Think *bigger*. In business, the number one reason most startup companies don't get off the ground isn't a lack of time or energy management. It's not even a lack of financial literacy. It's actually just *fear*. Remember, fear is a special emotion because it has the capacity to both paralyze and motivate us. When we are afraid to fail, we create limiting beliefs in ourselves and in our capabilities. Fearful thinking stifles big ideas and prevents us from imagining how we can turn a simple business idea into a unicorn (in business, a unicorn is a billion-dollar company). If you've got an idea for a business, you should want to see it become a unicorn, but it can only get there if you learn to think big. How can you amp up your thoughts and ideas by ten times? Or better yet, by fifty times? Turning big ideas into big businesses takes time, but in reality, if you're going to start a business, why not make your goal to have that business be the biggest and best business it can be? To put things in context, as I've mentioned, I've completed my share of marathons and half marathons, and what I've learned is this: Running a marathon *isn't* double the energy of running a half marathon. It takes the same amount of effort for me to get myself up early, put on my shoes, and get outside to run. The amount of additional effort is incremental once I've committed to the idea of running. The only thing that changes is how far I have to run, but if I'm already out there doing it, why not just go the full distance? In the same way, our time on earth is so limited that it would be foolish not to see how far one idea can take us.

Work your mindset

A huge step in taking action is learning to stop playing the victim card. If you're determined to thrive, stop telling yourself you're a victim. Perhaps more important, stop telling other people that you're a victim. Psychologically, people love playing the victim card because it gives them what they want (praise, empathy, adoration, support, etc.) without having to put in any effort. The danger is that when you tell yourself you're a victim, and when you allow yourself to ruminate on those low-frequency vibrations and the negative feelings that come with it, you will create a reality that reflects that.

For months after my divorce, I felt like a victim because I had to pay out 40 percent of my income in alimony. But I quickly realized that if I changed my mindset and focused on growing my income, the percentage of my earnings I was paying in alimony would be considerably less. And that's exactly what I did, and suddenly I didn't feel like I was a victim of my divorce.

So, when it comes to manifesting, keep your sights set on your success and don't be a victim of anything. I mean it—not the economy or a recession or even your own failure. Remember, during the Great Depression, the unemployment rate in the United States was around 20 percent, the highest it had ever been. That sounds scary, but if we just reframe it slightly and say that 80 percent of Americans were still working during the Great Depression, that sounds much more empowering.

You can empower yourself simply by not playing the victim. When you stop playing the victim, you give yourself back the power that comes with being accountable for things in your own life. Viktor Frankl, a Jewish-Austrian psychiatrist and Holocaust survivor, spent three years of his life in four different concentration camps. During his time as a prisoner, he witnessed hundreds of people around him perish under Nazi rule, including his parents and his wife. By all accounts, Frankl was a victim, but he never succumbed to that label. It was his belief that the Nazis could do anything to him—torture him, take away his clothes, his food, his family, and his self-dignity—but they could never take away his power to choose his response. Frankl's mindset helped him persevere, because it allowed him to be courageous in the face of hardship and choose resilience over defeat.

If you do find yourself at a roadblock or a setback in life, view it as an opportunity to pivot. Whether it's losing your job, having to scrap an investment idea, or failing at your first, fifth, or tenth attempt at starting a business, always choose a response that empowers you. Perseverance is incredibly difficult, because it can't be taught in a self-help book; it can only be learned by getting up every time you fail. It takes hard work, and that can be intimidating and discouraging, but think of it this way: If you don't persevere in the face of failure, the problems that you don't resolve will ultimately become your limits when it comes to what you will achieve.

Exercise Your Knowledge

Regardless of what it is you're manifesting, turning desires into a reality takes intention, planning, and perseverance. Whether it's something relatively small or something potentially life-changing, the process is the same. That's because taking specific actions and putting in the necessary effort are essential to seeing the outcomes we want.

1. Think of something you want to manifest. It can be as big or as small as you want, as long as it's realistic.

2. Write down a list of actions you'd need to take to turn that want into a reality. Remember, be specific and

be comprehensive about these actions (the more steps, the better). They might include things like doing some research or spending time practicing a specific skill related to that goal.

3. Rate each of the actions on a scale of one to ten based on how much effort or hard work they would require to complete.

4. Consider the likelihood of you manifesting your goal without taking any of those actions.

5. Now consider the likelihood of you manifesting your goal if you were able to take all the necessary actions.

By breaking down your manifestation into steps like this, you'll be able to stay motivated by tackling one step at a time that moves you toward your goal.

CHAPTER 16

Increasing Your Capacity to Receive

One of the most profound things I've learned on my journey toward a life of abundance is the importance of shifting my mindset from one of *deserving* to one of *receiving*. When I left home, there was no safety net. I had to work to find jobs, secure contracts, and deliver on big projects by myself and *for* myself. If I didn't get things done, nobody else would. I made every decision myself, and I believed I was entitled to every single penny I made. At sixteen years old, my mindset went like this: *I earned it, so I deserve it*. If only life were that simple.

When we make a good decision that leads to a good outcome, we feel like we're entitled to the good stuff. But other times, good decisions lead to bad outcomes. For example, a dedicated entrepreneur who puts in long hours, takes calculated risks, and follows a well-thought-out business plan can still experience financial setbacks or challenges. Despite their commitment and hard work, external factors such as economic downturns, unexpected market

changes, or industry disruptions can impact their business negatively. That's why, if you're operating under the assumption that all
good decisions lead to good outcomes and you believe that you
deserve what comes to you, it's easy to feel like life isn't fair when
you wind up making a good decision that leads to an undesirable
outcome. When you don't receive what you think you deserve,
those feelings of entitlement lead to bitterness, which inhibits your
ability to feel gratitude—which, going back to the law of vibration, hurts your sense of self-worth and destroys your capacity to
create the life you want.

> **Lightbulb Moment:** If we shift from the egocentric belief
> of "I deserve this" to the belief of "I'm open to receiving
> whatever life offers me," we're able to accept difficult outcomes
> and expand our capacity to receive blessings we don't even
> necessarily believe we deserve.

I know I've spent a lot of time hammering home the fact that
it's necessary to sacrifice things and work hard for what you want
(because it *really* is). However, I've learned through my own experiences that, even though I'm working hard for what I want, there are
limits to what I can control. I believe that there is a greater power in
the universe that exists to bless our lives. Whether you call it God or
luck or chance is your prerogative, but at the end of the day, we have
to accept that things happen in life over which we have little control.

It's human nature to want to believe that we're in full control of
our lives, but realistically we are only in control of the choices we
make. As far as our efforts go, they don't always correlate with the
outcome of things. Some opportunities you didn't plan for or manifest make their way into your path. When you believe that you're in

control of the outcomes in your life, you're tapping into the mindset of deserving, rather than receiving.

For me, this was a difficult but necessary lesson to learn. I used to struggle a lot with receiving, because giving to other people is a huge part of what fulfills me. As a father to my kids, a leader in my church, and a passionate businessman, I used to pride myself on being self-sufficient, strong, and independent. I liked that I could do anything I put my mind to without asking anybody for help. I suppose I believed, on some level, that asking others for help made me weak. I had to learn to surrender those beliefs and come to terms with the fact that I wasn't in control of everything. I didn't create *everything*.

When we put our aspirations and desires out into the Universe, it can take a little while to get a response. Sometimes we don't get the answer we're hoping for, but other times, the answer is better than we could have imagined. Likewise, it might take our whole lives to understand the answer, and sometimes we might have to ask multiple times.

Growing up in a single-parent household where money was tight, it was easy to compare my circumstances to my friends'. Unlike me, they all lived on the fancy side of town, in communities with big houses and recreational luxuries like basketball courts and swimming pools, but that wasn't the difference between our lives that stood out to me. What stood out to me was that all of my friends had two parents, and I only had *one*. *Where was* my *dad? Why don't I have a dad?* These questions weighed on me for years. My father was still alive, but he wasn't around, and I couldn't understand why. I thought about it all the time, praying about it, and asking whoever would listen to me why I had this gaping hole in my family.

With the benefit of hindsight, I can tell you that at such a young age, I didn't yet have the capacity in myself to receive the answer I was so desperately looking for. In fact, it wasn't until years—literally *decades*—later, when I had my own children, that I understood and had the capacity to receive an answer. Even if we're excellent at being givers, sometimes we have to carve out space in our lives to receive things from others. And that takes time. Now, when I look at my children, I know that it is a thousand times harder to be a parent without a child than to be a child without a parent. For the most part, I was fine without my dad, but as a parent, I can't fathom going a day without my kids. Receiving that answer has inspired me to be the best father I can be, but it's also allowed me to open up and be empathetic toward my own dad. Granted, he made some questionable choices, but now that I have the capacity to understand what he went through as a parent, I've been able to create space to receive that answer and make peace with it.

So, if you're reading this and you're feeling stuck on something right now, or if you're frustrated that you haven't gotten an answer to the question you keep asking, be patient. Do what you can to create space in your life to receive answers, and trust that when the time is right, you will.

Upper limits

Every single person has a unique "upper limit." Metaphorically, that limit represents whatever a person believes they deserve in life, including their job, wealth, friends, and even happiness. It makes sense that when people are below their limit, they'll always work up toward it. What might surprise you, though, is that when people are above their limit, they'll often find ways to self-sabotage to bring themselves back down to the "level" they think they deserve. People with a higher upper limit often have more self-worth or believe they deserve more than other people; they often take on new challenges with ease, get promoted more often, and make more money. On the other hand, people who live their whole lives inside their comfort zone will never experience the growth that comes with testing and expanding their upper limit. The good news is that your upper limit isn't rigid—you can change it.

✓ CHECK YOURSELF

Challenging your upper limit doesn't have to mean doing something rash like quitting your job to start a new business. Here are several smaller ways you can change your upper limit:

- Talk to like-minded people.
- Learn a new skill.
- Read an article about something you find interesting but know nothing about.
- Identify patterns in your life that don't serve you and then learn how to break them.
- Reframe new challenges as opportunities for growth.

When it comes to changing our upper limit, we all have our own version of a Plimsoll line. This is a visible line all passenger and cargo ships have along the side of the vessel. This mandatory line serves as a reference mark for the maximum water level to which a fully loaded ship can be considered safely immersed. Knowing the exact Plimsoll line is essential to determining the ship's upper limit and ensures the ship is not overloaded or at risk of capsizing. The Plimsoll line can change, depending on factors like how heavy the ship's cargo is and the density of the water the ship will be sailing through.

As with ships, our personal Plimsoll line represents the upper limit of our safety or comfort zone—usually in the form of our self-imposed beliefs about what we can achieve or how happy we can be. These limiting beliefs can hold us back from reaching our full potential and experiencing true fulfillment. By identifying where the upper limit of our comfort zone is, we can learn to expand it and eventually even overcome it. But changing our upper limit doesn't need to be dramatic or sudden. Gradual changes can transform how we live our lives and broaden our capacity to receive abundantly. When you take steps toward expanding your own comfort zone and embrace the discomfort that comes with it, you're able to improve your capability to receive and will feel more confident in your ability to tackle other challenges you come across down the road. With practice, you can learn to flex your upper limit so you can take on new tasks when necessary and still be able to return to your comfort zone level.

Receive with an open hand

So, how does this relate to finance? Well, your unique mental script, financial personality, and the choices you make toward your financial fitness all contribute to your ability to meet and exceed your financial upper limit. That includes things like your earning potential. If you don't believe you're worthy of a raise, you're not going to get one because you'll never ask for one. If you don't tell yourself that not only can you be a CEO, but you can be the *best* CEO there ever was, you'll never be bold enough to find out.

The parable of the drowning man tells the story of a devout Christian man who refuses help from three different rescuers, telling each of them, "I don't need your help. God is going to save me." When he inevitably dies and gets to heaven, he angrily asks God,

"Why didn't you come and rescue me?" God smiles at him and says, "Well, I sent you three different rescuers, and you didn't accept help from any of them." This story drives home the point that opportunities, whether financial, professional, or personal, are often right in front of us, but if we aren't open to receiving them and playing an active role in seizing them, we'll drown while waiting to be rescued.

In such a competitive world, it's easy to believe that to be successful, you have to hustle. And that's true to some extent. Sometimes, though, if you're wrapped up in being productive and don't find the time among the busyness of business to open up to receiving things, you'll miss out on opportunities that present themselves to you when you are still. As someone who likes to stay busy, I've found that I receive the most from life when I sit back and create space for opportunities to reveal themselves to me.

For example, I dedicated most of my time while I was on sabbatical to creating my own podcast, *Strategic Financial Leadership*. I had the privilege of interviewing a few dozen brilliant people, and on one specific episode, the guest I was interviewing happened to mention that he had just moved from New York City to Boulder, Colorado. At the time, I lived about a sixty-minute drive from where he lived. Typically, I wouldn't drive that far for a meeting if I could just simply chat with someone over the phone, but in the spirit of pushing my upper limit, I insisted on making the time to meet up in person.

A few weeks later, I drove to Boulder to meet him at his office. We got to talking about work and life, business and passions, and to cut a long story short, within a couple of months I was the new CFO of his company. Just like that. Just by pushing my upper limit a little more, I was able to receive tenfold. I didn't become the CFO overnight or by being *passive*, but if I hadn't developed the capacity to receive from others, I wouldn't have been open to taking that chance and meeting him at his office. And if I'd been too busy work-ing and grinding and focusing on doing my own thing to get out of my comfort zone, I would've missed out entirely on the opportunity to learn new things and grow.

I truly believe that if our cup is empty, we cannot pour into the cups of others and be an agent for good in their lives. If we make sure that our own cup runneth over first and are open to receiving abundantly, we will have the capacity to give generously to those around us.

As an adult, I'm still working on being comfortable receiving from others, but I distinctly remember my first experience of hav-ing my cup overflow with blessings given to me by others. As the result of an ugly divorce in my childhood, my mom, along with me and four of my siblings, moved from a spacious house in Parker, Colorado, into an unfinished two-bedroom house in Cottonwood. It looks a lot different today, but in the 1990s, Cottonwood was a dingy, unkempt little neighborhood in Parker, and the house we lived in was equally unkempt. My three brothers and I shared the two bedrooms, and my mom shared the basement with my sister. They put down rugs over the concrete and separated the small space with bookshelves for privacy, but the situation was still far from ideal. Money was tighter than ever, and as a consequence, we struggled with food insecurity too.

Looking back, it was perhaps the peak of scarcity for my family, and scarcity weighed on everyone's minds, including mine. When our first Christmas in Cottonwood rolled around, we sat together, snuggled under blankets, and watched all the Christmas classics: *Frosty, How the Grinch Stole Christmas*, and my personal favorite, *Christmas Vacation*. We had no expectation of waking up to gifts under the tree or a big Christmas meal, but we knew that we were deeply loved and were grateful to have one another.

As we were enjoying our family time, suddenly the doorbell rang. I wrapped my blanket round my shoulders and shuffled over to the door. When I opened it, there was nobody there. My immediate thought was a bitter one: Had we seriously been ding-dong ditched? On Christmas Eve? I shook my head in disgust and turned around to shut the door.

That's when I saw it: a large box sitting on our front step with a label addressed to our family. Who on earth had left that for us? I poked my head out and peered around. There was nobody anywhere near our house. I was perplexed and a little intrigued as I rushed to bring the box inside. I put it in the middle of the living room so everyone could see it and pulled open the lid with nervous excitement. To my sheer delight, inside the box were six gifts, individually wrapped and addressed to each of us. Mine was a Lego set, which was my absolute favorite as a kid, and one of my brothers, who was super into sports, unwrapped a baseball. It was clear that whoever had left this box of goodies knew exactly what each of us would like.

It was the most touching gesture I'd ever received, but it didn't stop there. Fifteen minutes later, the doorbell rang again. This time, we all raced to the door to find yet *another* box of gifts to unwrap. A few minutes after that, the doorbell rang again, and then *again*. This went on for hours, until we'd unwrapped upward of a dozen gifts.

To answer the question I'm sure you're wondering about: No, it wasn't Santa Claus, but it was the closest I've come to experiencing a true Christmas miracle. This incredible act of kindness had been thoughtfully arranged by our new church community to help give our family a most special Christmas. To be clear, and I can't stress this enough, it wasn't the gifts that made it so memorable; it was the fact that people had gone out of their way during the busiest season of the year to give their time and their love to our family. I never could have imagined something so gracious happening, but that Christmas changed my life. We certainly weren't expecting it, but it showed me that if we are open to receiving good things, or if we expect that things will work themselves out, eventually they do.

Receiving isn't about getting what we think we're entitled to; in fact, it doesn't even have to mean tangible things. We can receive grace, friendships, opportunities, ideas, compassion, growth, and even fulfillment by focusing less on what we think we're entitled to and more on having gratitude for blessings in life that happen unexpectedly. When we shift our mindset to being open to receiving and do away with the belief that we control every outcome, we allow ourselves to *expect* that things will work out. And when we *expect* that good things will happen in life, we will manifest them into existence by taking those chances, pushing our limits, and creating the reality we want. Miracles are often people pouring from their overflowing cup, and it's important to know when and how to receive from others so we in turn can bless the lives of those around us.

I'm a big fan of the phrase "You cannot receive with a closed hand," because it emphasizes the idea that receiving and giving are so deeply intertwined. When we give to others, we must do it with open hands. When we do this, we allow ourselves to be open to receiving from others. It also highlights an important nuance, which is that we don't necessarily have to give others the same things we receive. We may be equipped to give large amounts of money, but not much time, or vice versa. The bottom line is that it's difficult to live a truly financially abundant life without practicing both giving and receiving in some capacity.

The French term *noblesse oblige* is another fitting expression that describes the implicit responsibility that those who are privileged have a duty to treat those who are less fortunate with generosity and nobility. Over their lifetime, the twenty-five most generous donors in the United States have donated close to $200 billion to philanthropy work, charities, and causes they are passionate about, but you certainly don't need to have millions of dollars to be able to give to others. If you don't have the capacity to donate money, give your time, your love, your talents, and your support, and you will receive growth, happiness, gratitude, and fulfillment tenfold in return.

Be an agent for good

Lastly, I want to reemphasize how increasing your capacity to receive can help you be an agent for good. Being an agent for good is crucial in this world, because we are conditioned to believe that there isn't *enough* and the world is a place of scarcity rather than abundance. Growing up, I thought the world was full of scarcity, but now I can see just how much life has to offer me, and a huge part of that has come from practicing giving and receiving.

Ever since that Christmas in Cottonwood, my approach to helping others and serving my community has changed. If you're at a place in life where you're constantly feeling bombarded with reports and articles with statistics about how the world is in dire straits and there's scarcity everywhere, my message to you is this: Be an agent for good. When you receive, take that mercy and that goodness and go out and bless the lives of other people. You don't have to volunteer at a soup kitchen, take it upon yourself to start a charity, or solve world hunger. Being an agent for good means starting with the little things.

Stop focusing on doing what's *good* and start focusing on doing what's *best*. Find out ways that you can bless your loved ones, friends, and community. It's possible that some people might not know they need help, or they might not know how to ask for it, but if we can figure out what it is people need from us, we'll be much better equipped to give it to them.

Sometimes, you might find it's not *what* they need us to give them, but rather *who* they need us to be *for* them. It could be as simple as being a gentle friend during a dark time, or giving someone the supportive silence they need to work through things. Whatever it is, when we're able to give time to the small gestures that lighten people's loads, we're putting positive vibrations out into the world that will bless others and, in turn, attract more positive vibrations to us and the abundant possibilities that come with them.

I'm sure you're wondering what the catch is, and there is a small caveat that comes with being an agent for good. Here it is: Don't put the needs of others above your own means. Helping others is an important part of being an agent for good, but making sure you're not giving more than you can afford to (physically, emotionally, and financially) is paramount. If someone you know needs help paying their bills, but you're struggling to pay your own mortgage, it would be harmful to your own financial fitness to offer them financial help. So, even if you're presented with an opportunity to help those in need and you have the desire to help them, be sure you're being realistic about the extent and type of support you're able to offer them.

🧠 Exercise Your Knowledge

Take a moment to reflect on something you've done recently that positively affected someone else's life. Whom did you help? How did they respond? Now, consider whether your action was good, better, or best for that scenario. If it was good, what could you have done differently that might have been better for them? What's the *best* possible thing that you could have done?

CHAPTER 17

Working on Your Relationship with Yourself

R egardless of where you start, the most important relationship you'll encounter on your journey to an abundant and fulfilling life is the relationship you have with yourself. As cliché as that sounds, our capacity to show up for other people is directly proportional to how committed we are to showing up for ourselves.

> **Lightbulb Moment:** It is possible to be an agent for good and still put yourself first. In fact, it's *necessary*, because giving yourself time to recenter and check in with your own well-being ensures that you can give attention to others generously and meaningfully.

The world is a phenomenally busy place, and over the last fifty consecutive years, people have reported feeling busier than the year before. This is a trend that is unlikely to slow down or reverse anytime soon. Between studying or working, having relationships, raising kids, and doing chores, it can feel like there isn't time left for much else. If we add in time spent being an agent for good and helping others, our spare time becomes even more limited, and that's before we've even thought about making time to look after our health, spend time on our hobbies and passions, or sleeping!

Part of this feeling of being perpetually rushed comes from the fact that as economies grow and people become wealthier, time literally becomes more valuable. Suddenly, an hour of time is worth double what it was a few years ago, so we feel more pressured to pack as much productivity into that hour as possible. But what if I told you that you could increase your productivity by spending more time taking care of yourself? Sounds too good to be true, right? Well, it's not. A US survey found that for people who practiced self-care in any capacity, two-thirds reported being more productive, and some 70 percent reported feeling happier than those who did not engage in self-care.[1] To know yourself deeply and truthfully means you have taken the time to practice self-awareness and self-acceptance, both of which are vital to realizing and achieving whatever you were put on this planet for.

Taking time to reflect and introspect allows you to ground yourself, feel a sense of belonging on earth, and ensures you're in tune with your core values so you're always thinking, feeling, and acting in accordance with whatever your bigger goals are. Make the time to focus on yourself a nonnegotiable, because if you don't, I guarantee you will find a million little things to distract you from working on your relationship with yourself, and that's a dangerous habit you don't want to become a routine.

Selfish versus self-oriented

I'm a zealous, independent go-getter, and I *love* it. From a distance though, I can understand why people might misattribute my incessant busyness to being selfish rather than just self-oriented. In business and in life, I've found that a lot of people don't really understand the difference, so it's important to make the distinction clear. *Selfishness* is the inability to recognize the needs of others because you are focused on fulfilling your own needs. Being *self-oriented* means that you prioritize doing what you need to get done, but you still have the ability to recognize the needs of others and are aware of your capacity to help them with their own goals when you're able.

People often incorrectly assume that doing things for yourself is selfish, and therefore, doing anything that takes away from your ability to help others means you are a selfish person. But that couldn't be further from the truth. People who frequently give time to themselves have more confidence, higher self-esteem, and a greater sense of self-worth. It's really no surprise, then, that these individuals also have better relationships, are generally happier, and are more productive with the time they spend on other people. Just like the overflowing cup analogy, while it's good to help others, and it's important to remember that you exist in a world filled with other people who all have their own unique stories, struggles, and triumphs, nobody expects you to be the hero that rescues everyone else. When it comes to being self-oriented, you must strike a balance between being focused on your own needs, wants, and desires and also recognizing you're not the center of the entire universe.

So, what exactly are selfish behaviors, and how do they differ from self-oriented behaviors? In my opinion, allowing ourselves to be distracted by small, often meaningless things that get in the way of our being able to focus on our goals (however big or small) is selfish. It's not selfish to say no to helping your neighbor move, or canceling plans with friends because you need to prioritize an evening of quiet reflection, or holding off on responding to emails until you've had time to think about your answer, or limiting how much time you spend on social media. Saying no to things is an important part of making sure you're managing your time and energy wisely. Saying no to these things isn't selfish because, at their core, they take time away from what you might spend on doing the most important thing you're here on earth to do—whatever it may be.

What *is* a selfish behavior, then? I believe that selfishness is *not* writing the book you're meant to write, *not* starting the business that you're supposed to start, and even *not* being conscious of building savings now so your future self is financially secure. In my book, it's more selfish to turn away from the things you're good at and the talents you have, because not following those drivers will keep you from doing something truly remarkable that could have a huge impact on someone else's life. If you lose sight of doing the big-picture thing you're going to be remembered for doing, that's what is truly selfish.

For example, my purpose in life (at least right now) is to write this book because I have a unique perspective on something I know other people will benefit from. My goal is to help people get a better understanding of their finances, learn how to be financially fit, and lead abundant lives of their own. If I allow myself to be caught up in doing the small things, like helping out every single person I meet, or volunteering all of my spare time to just doing what is *good*, I'll miss out on my opportunity to share my passion for the thing I'm *best* at and can help others be better at too. I don't have to become completely selfish and cast aside the obligations I have to my clients, employees, and my family until I'm done working on my own thing. It's possible for me to make time for the needs of those around me yet not be consumed by their lives entirely. That's the difference between selfishness and self-orientation, and at the end of the day, when we aren't creating, building, and growing in the ways we're supposed to, in the ways that will get us to our goals and to true fulfillment, that's what is *truly* selfish.

> ## ✓ CHECK YOURSELF
>
> When it comes to being productive, you need to learn to distinguish between actions or behaviors that are selfish and those that are self-oriented. Simply put, selfish behaviors are those that hinder your ability to be productive. In other words, those behaviors don't serve an immediate or significant function. Off the top of your head, you might think of examples like binge-watching TV, aimlessly scrolling through social media, engaging in gossip or negative conversations, or even being a people pleaser. While these things can feel stimulating, what they have in common is that they don't serve a true purpose and are keeping you from spending time doing what is truly important. The next time you start doing something that's going to take up a considerable amount of time, ask yourself:
>
> - Does doing this activity serve a purpose?
> - Does doing this activity serve my purpose?
>
> Knowing the difference can help you prioritize your time and ensure you're always acting in accordance with your core values and your higher goals.

Protect your time

When it comes to prioritizing your time and energy, I'm not saying you should never, ever socialize. Having meaningful, supportive relationships matters without a doubt, but be mindful of where and how you spend your time and energy. My personal rule is if it's not a "heck yeah!" response, then it's actually a "no thanks." We've been taught to be agreeable because it's the polite thing to do, but to avoid falling into the trap of distractions, it's actually important to be protective of your time.

People are usually (and understandably) protective of their wealth, because it's easy to identify periods of scarcity when it comes to money. When that happens, we usually feel compelled to change our behavior to compensate for the fact that our money is scarce. What surprises me, though, is that as a society, we often overlook how limited our time is. When you think about it, time is the scarcest resource of all: It can't be bought, sold, or earned at a job. It can't be bartered or traded for, and to a large extent, you can't be sure how much of it you have left until it's all gone. Where money and time are similar, though, is that you can *invest* in both however you want. But you have to be careful, because if you only have a small amount of time left, how you spend it *matters*.

I described this exact notion to the audience at a conference where I was giving a keynote speech about designing a purpose-driven life. I took a step away from the podium and pulled out two simple props: a ball of twine and a pair of scissors. I was close to forty years old at the time, so I measured out about forty inches of twine and held it out lengthways between my thumbs and index fingers: one inch for every year an average man my age had left to live.

You can probably see where I'm going with this. Slowly, I started cutting off inches of string that represented all the years of time we typically spend doing activities like working, commuting, sleeping, and eating. Pretty soon my piece of twine was about half its size, but I kept going, cutting off more inches for the time spent socializing, doing chores, going to church or other community events, and spending time tending to the needs of loved ones.

A few people chuckled nervously as more and more pieces fell to the floor. By the time I was done, I had cut off all but about four inches of string. "That's all the time we really have left to do something that leaves an imprint on the world," I said, as a pensive silence filled the auditorium.

Bringing this to your attention can be daunting and uncomfortable, but my point is that the time we have to find and fulfill our purpose is limited. So, if you want to go after something in this life, do it, and do it *big*. Be committed, tenacious, and focused, and don't stop working at it until you get there.

Protect your attention

In his book *How to Fly a Horse*, visionary technologist Kevin Ashton describes how anyone can create anything.[2] He emphasizes the importance of taking small steps, learning from repetitive trial and error, and recognizing that the only guarantee of failure is to give up on something entirely. He believes that ordinary or everyday thinking has the capacity to create the truly remarkable, but he warns that creativity is easily stifled in an increasingly distractible world. Like him, I believe that everyone has the ability to do remarkable things, but on top of the passion, it takes discipline and focus, which often comes with making sacrifices and saying no to distractions.

Picture this: You've just sat down at your desk or office space to get some work done, when suddenly you see your phone light up on the desk beside you. Immediately, almost unconsciously, you reach for it to check your messages. It's one of your colleagues asking if you're interested in hanging out after work. You don't want to leave them hanging, so you respond with a yes to let them know you're in.

Then it occurs to you that you aren't exactly sure where the place they want to meet is located. So, you pick up your phone again to check the location, and just as you're doing that, a Facebook notification pops up, so you quickly check that too. (*I just want to get rid of the notification*, you tell yourself. *Those are so distracting*.) You open up the Facebook app, and before you know it you've been sucked into a scrolling spiral and you're looking at photos of your former neighbor's stepdaughter's boyfriend's family vacation. It's been an hour, and you still haven't accomplished what you set out to do.

If that sounds like you, you're not alone. But why are we so easily persuaded by distractions? Humans are hardwired to tune in to "new" information. It helped our ancestors detect potential threats and was a huge advantage when life was generally more dangerous. It also triggers a pleasure response in the brain known as the dopamine pathway (a.k.a. the feel-good hormone). Our brains simply love to look at and listen to new stimuli, which is why as soon as something new comes into our attention field (even if it's not particularly exciting), we are compelled to give it our full attention. The danger is that, in the digital age when social media and advertising are so readily accessible, it's easier than ever to engage with potential distractions that can overload our brains, distract our thought process, and hinder our ability to think and behave productively.

To a large extent in our society and the broader global economy, the main capital people are buying and selling is *focus*. From entrepreneurs to app developers to influencers, they all want the same thing: your attention. And for the most part, they are doing a pretty good job of getting it. Don't be misled; our attention is highly valuable. In fact, in a lot of ways, our attention is what drives the economy. Sellers are always competing for our attention because whatever their product is, they want our focus to be on looking at it, desiring it, and eventually *purchasing* it over someone else's.

While distraction is virtually impossible to avoid, scientists have identified one possible way of curbing how often and for how long we get distracted—and it's so simple that it just might work: Pay more attention. Our mind is like a muscle we must learn to train and focus. The first step in achieving a goal, be it investing, running a marathon, or anything in between, is focusing your mind. Tiny little distractions will get in your way if you let them, so knowing how to avoid them is crucial for staying focused on your higher purpose.

A study done by the psychology faculty at Harvard University found that you can actually train your brain to avoid distractions in just three simple steps.[3] First, learn to recognize when you're getting distracted. It might help to set up cues to remind you to notice when distractions are happening. For example, check in with yourself every time you reach for your phone or open your computer to make sure your mind and attention are focused on what you need to get done. Second, practice shifting your attention to the present moment to help reorient yourself in the here and now. Third, learn to savor the moment and pay attention to all the little details that ground you and keep you connected to whatever mission you've set out to accomplish. Doing these three things will help you feel less stress, be more grateful, and even make you a more productive creator.

Protect your boundaries

Now I want to highlight an important lesson *you* need to go out and teach to those around you: your unique code. You're thinking, *What the heck is that, Steve?* Each of us has a unique code or set of boundaries that needs to be in place so we can function optimally. These boundaries might be verbal or nonverbal, and they can differ from person to person, but essentially, showing others your unique code means telling them how you operate and how they can get the best out of you.

My kids love to go ten-pin bowling, but because they're still young, they always ask me to put up the lane boundaries so their bowling balls don't fall into the gutters. For them, having those boundaries makes them better bowlers, and while it might be a bit of a stretch, it's a good metaphor for how boundaries can affect our performance as adults. Adults need boundaries, too, but because everyone has their own unique code, everyone has different boundaries we need to be aware of. Remember, these boundaries aren't always permanent, but when they're necessary, they should be respected.

Long before I became a businessman, I'd engage with people who would do things that really rubbed me the wrong way, and instead of talking it out, I'd ignore them, or worse, I'd lash out at them, sometimes at the cost of the relationship. Now, by being vocal about what my boundaries are and making myself aware of other people's codes, I'm able to work through difficult times, recognize what other people need to function optimally, and get back to a state of productive peace. It can be difficult to be transparent with people who don't know what your code is, but just like saying no to lending people money, the more you practice telling people your unique code, the easier it is to enforce the boundaries you need.

Your unique code might change depending on what your relationship is to someone. For example, your boundaries will be different for your spouse, kids, friends, and colleagues, and *they* will certainly have different boundaries too. It all comes back to understanding that while you *do* matter, so does everyone else. To a large extent, those boundaries are there to ensure that nobody oversteps or infringes on someone else's ability to function optimally.

Putting up boundaries for ourselves is a way to protect ourselves from others *and* protect others from us. Sometimes we need boundaries to be able to be there for other people when they need us. It's possible that your boundary to indicate whether someone respects and cares about you is that they just give you space. It sounds counterintuitive, but that's how boundaries work.

Tell people how they should treat you, and then let them know when they overstep. When people do cross your boundaries (and they might), it's important to tell them how you feel. As a man of faith, I believe it's important to extend people grace and forgive them. I think it's possible to give people second chances, and even *second* second chances, because no one is perfect, and if someone matters enough to you, they should be given a fair opportunity to change their behavior. Give people a chance to learn your code and understand what your boundaries are, and if they show you that they do, that's great.

On the other hand, if they don't, it might be time to consider enforcing a more distinct boundary. When it comes to relationships out in the real world, whether it's in your personal life or at work, there are things you can't just walk away from. You can't just ghost people or ice them out of the relationship; you need to speak up. If you don't, you're unlikely to be heard. You shouldn't be malicious or condescending, but saying something as simple as "Hey, it would mean a lot to me if you did this moving forward" can go a long way. Explaining *why* or *how* someone overstepped your boundary can help make sure they don't repeat that behavior in future.

For example, something I can't stand is being spoken over or interrupted when I'm speaking. I know I'm not alone when it comes to that pet peeve, but it's particularly important to know how to handle it in my line of work. When I first started out and was giving a lot of presentations, I had to learn how to communicate that boundary with my team. I'd often say, "When you spoke over me in that presentation, it made me feel like you were taking credit for my work. I have a lot of respect for your ideas, but I'd really appreciate it if next time you could let me finish what I'm saying before you step in and give your thoughts." I wasn't disrespectful, but I was clear about what I needed from them to behave optimally. It would have been disrespectful to not say anything at all and just sulk over the situation. On top of that, not communicating or respecting boundaries fosters negative emotions, which leads to bad vibrations and ultimately hinders productivity.

Extend grace to yourself

If it seems like we've digressed from strategies and frameworks of financial fitness, that's kind of the point. While we can work tirelessly at applying strategies and commit to doing everything according to the six drivers of financial fitness model, the bottom line is this: We are never going to be financially fit, achieve financial security, have financial freedom, or live a life of abundance *unless* we focus on ourselves, set boundaries, and learn to avoid interruptions.

Starting with having a good relationship with yourself and recognizing how valuable your time is will ensure you're allocating it appropriately, particularly when it comes to focusing on achieving your goals. You may not realize it, but how you perceive yourself trickles into every other aspect of your life, including whether your mindset is geared toward expecting and receiving versus earning and deserving. When you're focused on earning and deserving, you're inclined to believe you're a bad person simply because bad things happen to you, but that simply isn't true. The truth is, sometimes bad things happen when we *don't* deserve them, and it sucks. It's okay to acknowledge when things suck, but it's important to not let it define you, because sometimes you receive things you don't deserve either, and that's okay too.

Why am I so passionate about getting this message across that I dedicated an entire chapter to it? Well, because I know that most people have a difficult time being alone with themselves. Even though we may be good at giving, it's important to recognize the benefit of receiving from others. We might be good at forgiving others, but it's necessary to learn to extend grace to ourselves just as often as we offer it to others. Practicing self-awareness and self-acceptance is the key to having a good relationship with yourself, and that is the foundation of being a productive, self-oriented person.

Hopefully by now, the importance of working on your relationship with yourself is clear. It is impossible to be an agent for good for others if you aren't confident and satisfied in who you are. Knowing how to identify when you're being selfish is necessary, but so is giving yourself permission to do things that are self-oriented. So, help others when you can, but be cautious about how quickly you commit to taking time away from yourself to do things that might just be *good* things rather than the *best* things. Saying no to distractions means saying yes to respecting yourself, yes to productivity, and yes to fulfillment!

Exercise Your Knowledge

Think of a time when someone overstepped one of your boundaries. How did you react? Communicating what your boundaries are with friends, family members, or colleagues can be intimidating and might even feel a bit awkward, particularly if it's someone you're close to. With that in mind, it's important to remember that people can and do make mistakes, so reacting in a way that reinforces what your boundary is but doesn't jeopardize the relationship can be important. If that's the case, instead of jumping into a heated argument, try using the three P's method: point, pause, and possible solutions.

Here's an example:

1. **Point**. Express how you're feeling in the moment. Be specific and conscious. Also, remember to use *I* statements when defining your point (e.g., "I felt frustrated when you cut me off before I finished speaking because it makes me feel like you don't care about my feelings when I express them.").

2. **Pause**. Give the person time to respond, listen to what they have to say, and then respond by saying something like "Thank you for taking the time to listen to me." If you still feel upset, it's okay to ask for more time. Try saying something like "I'm going to need a minute because I'm feeling frustrated. I'm getting really defensive, and I feel like this conversation is not productive. I don't want to hurt you, so I need a few minutes to organize my thoughts."

3. **Possible Solution**. Offer a possible solution that is rooted in helping them understand how you want to be treated in the future. Remember, we need to teach people what our unique code is; they can't just figure it out as they go. You could say, "It would really make me feel better if you did *this* moving forward." Then, explain to them what your code is and give them an opportunity to change the way they behave. If they continue to behave in a way that compromises your feelings, then it might be time to consider setting sterner boundaries.

CHAPTER 18

Asking Better Questions

I've asked you to think about *a lot* of questions so far—from small, simple ones like "What does financial freedom mean to you?" to the much more complex ones like "What is your purpose here on earth and how can you fulfill it?" Perhaps you've managed to answer a few of these questions along the way, and if you haven't, my hope is that you've at least learned to be comfortable with searching inside yourself for honest answers. When we practice self-inquiry by asking thoughtful questions, we are taking the time to understand ourselves more deeply and find ways in which we might still be able to grow.

> **Lightbulb Moment:** There is tremendous power in asking good questions. Why? Because asking good questions leads us to good answers. It's that simple.

Just like the old saying "Listen to understand, not to respond," there is great importance in knowing *how* to ask meaningful questions. Often, I see people making the mistake of asking questions to give a response rather than to understand the person to whom they're speaking. Asking a question to start a dialogue with someone is perfectly fine, but if you're asking a question you already know the answer to just so you can respond with your own input, you're jeopardizing the opportunity to make a genuine connection with someone else.

Think back to when I asked you to reflect on your current place in life. I mentioned that there are roughly eight billion other people sharing this planet with us. That's eight billion individuals with their own beliefs, values, unique abilities, and goals. Along with that, they also have their own relationships, obstacles, failures, and triumphs. Just as you have a remarkable purpose inside you waiting to be discovered, every single other person has their own purpose and their own unique story to tell. Yes, *you* matter, and you should feel passionately about sharing your talents with the world, but with that comes the responsibility to also give others the time and space to share theirs. Many people spend their lives chasing fortune and fame, not realizing that people (and our relationships with them) are immeasurably valuable. We have the capacity inside us to learn from and be inspired by one another, but to do that, we must first learn to understand others as deeply as we know ourselves.

Allow me to let you in on a little secret I've learned about relationships as a businessman: Genuine connection is not something you can fake. Read that sentence again. You *cannot* lie your way into a meaningful partnership. Whether it's an in-law, your kids, or a potential client, real connections require real effort. So, if you're wondering how to go about building more genuine relationships with the people in your lives, the answer is in the questions you ask. Be *genuinely* interested. Remember Oprah Winfrey's remark about the one question every guest she interviewed would ask her: *How did I do?* People *love* to feel important, and they love to be told that they matter, and one way to show them that they do is by asking questions that will help you understand what matters to them.

Power of asking questions

Cards on the table, I'm not perfect (spoiler alert: nobody is!). There have definitely been times in my life when I was more focused on business growth than personal growth, and during those times I was less inclined to spend time asking people questions. For the most part, though, I've been pretty good about it, because building strong, genuine connections with people is one of my *musts*. And the time I have spent working on strengthening my relationships with people and showing them I understand what matters to them has enabled me to get the most value out of my relationships. Throughout my adult life, I've made an effort to make asking questions a part of my everyday routine, but the desire to stay inquisitive was instilled in me long before I even left home.

My late Grandpa Clifford was a tremendous man. He is, without a doubt, one of my idols, and he was the person that first introduced me to the power of asking questions—even if I didn't really understand it at the time. One of my clearest memories is when I was about nine years old. We were living in California, and my siblings and I were outside playing in the summer heat. I decided to run inside to grab an ice pop to cool off.

From the kitchen, I could hear Grandpa Clifford visiting with my mom out in the living room, and before I even had time to grab my snack, I heard his husky voice calling for me. "Steven! Come on in here!"

Dang it! I was eager to get back outside to my game. But my mother raised me to be respectful, so I forfeited my snack and walked with childish reluctance into the living room.

Grandpa Clifford was leaning forward in his armchair, with an open hand reaching out to wave me over. Even at a young age, I knew there was something different about him. He always wore dress shirts with a front pocket, and everywhere he went, he brought a tiny ring-bound notebook filled with questions. This visit was no different. He sat me down on his knee, flipped through the pages in his notebook, scanning the questions for one he thought I might like. Then he turned to me and asked, "Steven, how big do you think the universe is?"

As a kid, these exchanges seemed completely arbitrary. He would ask me all sorts of random questions about politics, money, and life, but in retrospect, I realize that the reason he asked me all those questions was to learn about who I was. He wanted to know me and know how I thought and felt, even as a little kid. Asking me those questions helped him better understand how I saw the world, and I've carried that forward with me throughout my life.

I have a great deal of appreciation and admiration for him. It wasn't just me though; he would ask these questions of anyone who would answer him. He was always inquisitive, and he taught me how to be curious.

It wasn't until I overheard a friend of mine introduce me to someone as "Steve, the guy who likes to ask a lot of hard-hitting questions" that I realized just how profound of an impact my grandpa had had on me. I am beyond grateful for Grandpa Clifford and his notebook, and the lesson he taught me about the importance of asking meaningful questions.

I don't want to exaggerate, but now, between my family, colleagues, clients, and anyone in between, I think I ask upward of one hundred questions a day. In fact, I love asking questions so much that I created a podcast, *Boost Your Financial IQ,* as a platform where I can indulge in asking as many questions as I possibly can and share the knowledge and insights I receive from the answers with others. Teaching others what I know about financial fitness is a huge part of fulfilling my purpose, but adjusting my focus from sharing my knowledge with the world to being the inquirer and harnessing my ability to understand what matters to other people has completely changed the way I live my life.

I've had the privilege of meeting, interviewing, and working with some incredible people, but I didn't learn about their unique stories and abilities by incessantly talking about myself. Instead, I learned to ask people how we could get the most value out of our conversations. Asking good questions also connects back to the importance of starting with empathy. When we show enthusiasm for our relationships with others, making genuine connections with them becomes effortless, and in that way, we can better understand how to use the time we have with them to the best of our ability. This doesn't just apply to professional relationships, though. Taking an interest in understanding what matters to your friends, family, and even people in your wider community will ensure you're able to identify the abundance of experiences and opportunities these connections can offer you *and* show up for them by being an agent for good in their lives.

From a social perspective, the importance of making sure we're taking an interest in others and asking meaningful questions is obvious: People are interested in people who are interested in them. This symbiotic social connection is the foundation of making genuine relationships, but asking questions has physiological benefits too. As we discussed in chapter 14, asking open-ended questions improves the brain's ability to solve problems. When we ask complex questions (of ourselves or other people), our brains are primed to enter a state of in-depth reflection as we contemplate our response. When this happens, our brains get totally fired up, with multiple regions of our brains that otherwise wouldn't be active at the same time engaging. If we regularly practice asking open-ended, complex questions, over time, our brain cell networks start to rewire themselves, making new connections that allow us to gather information from all over the brain, enhance our critical thinking skills, and help us answer these complex questions. So, if you thought asking questions was just some New Age nonsense, think again, because the premise that asking questions has the power to change your life is scientifically founded.

Reframing your questions

If you want to change your life *today*—as in right now—the best piece of guidance I can offer you is this: Ask better questions. If you're already asking questions and aren't satisfied with the answers you're receiving, try asking different questions. I said earlier that asking good questions leads us to good answers. Now, imagine the answers we could arrive at by asking even better questions, and even the *best* questions.

"Well, what constitutes a better question, Steve?" That in and of itself is a great question! Just as when we discussed how to increase our capacity to receive, when we put our aspirations and desires out into the Universe in the form of a question, sometimes it takes a while to get a response. Whether you're struggling to find an answer in your relationships or in business or in areas of personal growth, making sure you're asking the right questions can mean the difference between receiving the answer you want and getting no answer at all. Here's how: Whatever questions you ask yourself (or God or the Universe), your own subconscious mind is going to go to work to try and *solve* it for you. Neat, huh? Well, yes and no.

Are you asking questions like these:

- Why don't I have any money?

- Why can't I get a job?

- Why am I not successful?

- Why is life so unfair to me?

By asking these types of negative questions, what you're really doing is reinforcing the harmful beliefs that 1) you don't have money, 2) you can't get a job, 3) you're unsuccessful, and 4) life isn't fair. When you ask questions like these, you're triggering a mindset geared toward those fearful perceptions.

The catch here is that you cannot use that mindset to try and find solutions, because there aren't real solutions to questions that aren't *mobilizing*. Remember, what we fear, we fixate on, and what we hold in our minds, we manifest into our reality. People who frequently play the victim card often ask questions that are self-sabotaging and self-fulfilling, and that's why playing the victim never works out in anyone's favor.

On the other hand, what if you ask questions like these:

- What are some ways I can make more money?

- Where can I look for job openings in my field?

- How can I use the skills I have to create my own success?

- What day-to-day patterns can I do differently to align myself with my goals?

Now, you're asking empowering, stimulating questions that you and your mind *can* figure out.

> ## ✓ CHECK YOURSELF
>
> Remember, it's not always *what* you ask, but *how* you ask. Your subconscious mind has the incredible ability to solve problems in the background while you and the rest of your brain are working hard at doing other things. The caveat here is that while our minds are unbelievably powerful, they are also very susceptible to the information we provide. In other words, with great power comes great responsibility. And that responsibility is to ensure we are asking the right type of questions so our subconscious mind has the best chance at actually solving the problem.

Reframing the questions we ask ourselves is a powerful tool, and it's a technique I use in my personal life almost every single day. Rain or shine, I start my day by running, lifting weights, or doing some other form of exercise. In addition to the physical health benefits I reap from moving my body first thing in the morning, exercise gets my creative juices flowing. Before I start, though, I like to take a few minutes to meditate a little on the questions I'm currently seeking answers to. Sometimes they relate to my business ("How can I improve the user experience for people who visit my website?") and sometimes they're personal ("How can I have a closer relationship with my daughter?") When I start a run by asking those questions, I use my running time to reflect on them, and I let my mind go to work to try and find possible solutions. Asking powerful questions allows me to get out of my own head and be open to receiving whatever answers God has in store for me.

The bottom line here is that if you're going to tap into your subconscious mind's ability to solve problems, make sure you're asking thought-provoking questions that invite opportunities to reflect and *act*. Remember that our thoughts, feelings, and behaviors are all connected, so when we ask powerful questions that activate a mindset of abundance, we're more inclined to think and behave in ways that try to answer those very questions.

Let's say you're looking for a way to make more money. You might ask yourself, "What are some ways I can make more money?" While you're thinking about that, you might do a quick Google search that directs you to a podcast discussing five ways to grow wealth through passive income. The next thing you know, you're joining an accelerator program and creating a go-forward plan that outlines where you want to be in the next five years and what you need to do to get there. Just by reframing the question, you've managed to find an uncomplicated and practical solution.

I've said it before, but it bears repeating: Learning to ask better questions completely changed my life. When we seek to know ourselves, we learn to understand and have gratitude for our place in life, but when we seek to understand others, we quickly come to realize our true purpose on earth. I firmly believe that each and every one of us should strive to have better, deeper, and more meaningful relationships with ourselves as well as with those with whom we share our lives. There are an infinite number of connections, lessons, and solutions waiting for you. All you have to do is be bold enough to ask the questions and be open to receiving the answers. Regardless of whether it's in business, interpersonal connections, or your relationship with yourself, asking questions that empower you to *act* will expand your capacity to learn from others, better understand yourself, and maybe, just maybe, change your life like it did mine.

Exercise Your Knowledge

Making an effort to understand what matters to people goes a long way when forging meaningful relationships. Whether it's a pitch for a big business idea or a crucial conversation you need to have with someone, if you go into a situation wanting to truly connect with people, try starting the discussion with the following exercise:

1. Let the person know that making sure you understand what matters to them is a priority for you.

2. Outline what you think their priorities are.

3. Invite them to correct and expand on your assumptions where necessary.

Take a simple question you may ask your roommate, colleague, or spouse on a daily basis: How was your day? How many times have you asked someone that question out of routine politeness, and how often do you ask it because you're genuinely interested? Perhaps you've asked it because you're hoping someone will ask you the same question so you can offload some of the stressful things you've had to deal with throughout the day. I know I've done that at times, and I'm certain I'm not alone, but if we're able to home in on how to ask better questions, we can learn to make better connections with the people around us. I'm not saying you have to ask every person you'll ever meet a series of thought-provoking questions, but if we want to truly transform our lives, we must be mindful of the questions we ask *and* how we ask those questions.

CHAPTER 19

Harnessing a Mindset of Abundance

What does abundance look like? Depending on the context, abundance can be a tricky thing to visualize because it's inherently abstract. When I think of abundance, I imagine something big, without limits, that keeps on growing. The best way I can think of to visualize abundance is to think back to my Grandpa Clifford's question. For the last fourteen billion years, our universe has been expanding at an incomprehensible speed, even faster than the speed of light! To this day, scientists are still unsure of exactly how far the universe can expand, and when and if it will ever come to a stop. Now, we can't feel or see this expansion or perceive it in any way as we go about our days, but we know that it's out there. *Abundance* is out there in the same way.

If that makes you feel a little light-headed or tight in the chest, that's because humans are more comfortable thinking about things on a much smaller scale. So, let's shrink down for a moment from our amazing and expanding universe to our galaxy: the Milky Way. In addition to the sun and all the other planets that make up our solar system, there are more than one hundred billion stars in our galaxy, which already seems *unimaginably* vast. But our galaxy is actually just one of *billions* of other galaxies, each with their own stars, solar systems, and planets. Are you feeling eerily small yet? If your mind still isn't blown, scientists have estimated that there are around *one hundred quintillion* planets in our universe (if you're curious, that number looks like this when written out: 100,000,000,000,000,000,000). To me, this number visualizes abundance better than anything else on this planet—or any other planet for that matter!

> **Lightbulb Moment:** Scientists have hypothesized that there are likely more Earth-like planets that exist out there in our universe than there are grains of sand on the surface of our planet! If you've ever built a sandcastle on the beach, think of how many billions of grains of sand that one bucket can hold, and then think about the fact that that's just one bucket of sand from one beach, in one city, in one state, in one country, in one teeny tiny corner of the planet. That's not even counting all the sand in the Sahara Desert, which is roughly the same size as the whole of the United States.

Where am I going with all this talk about galaxies, silly-sounding numbers, and grains of sand? Well, it really boggles my mind to think about the fact that I can contemplate all the abundance that exists out there in our universe and still be controlled by the fear of scarcity in my own life.

Abundant resources

We create boundaries because they make us feel comfortable. We enjoy knowing where our limits are because we feel secure in our comfort zones. Finiteness exists within our minds. As a society, we have a limited capacity to think abundantly because we have been primed to believe that our world is full of rampant scarcity. The people who have abundant power in this world want the rest of the eight billion people to believe that there truly isn't abundance, when in reality, they are the ones who conjured up the concept of scarcity in the first place. Without scarcity, or at least the belief that there is scarcity, there is no power, and unfortunately that's what a lot of people are chasing after. Supply and demand form the foundation of economics, because if there were an abundance of things for everybody (money, jobs, material goods), there wouldn't be any chance to wield the power that comes from selling those things.

I'm probably going to get into trouble for sharing this with you, but when I was studying business strategy in college, the very first lesson they taught us was that resources are *finite*, and it was our job in business to find a way to optimize the resources we have. The premise makes sense on its face, because the entire business of marketing hinges on companies' ability to capitalize on the fear of scarcity. I even went around teaching businesses the same thing when I consulted for them. And sure, resources like gold, diamonds, and even oil in the ground are finite, but in reality, there *is* an abundance of possibilities to find other resources. Who knows what kinds of marvelous minerals and molecules there are in the depths of the ocean or growing on a tree in a remote area of the Amazon? So we shouldn't be afraid of the limitedness of things, because the number of other undiscovered resources is infinite.

When we think small, we think with a scarcity mindset, and we become fearful of the limits we set for ourselves. Those limits then become our comfort zone, and unless we are prepared to expand that comfort zone, we will always create a reality that reflects that mindset.

When I consult businesses that think they have a spending problem, nine times out of ten what they really have on their hands is an earning problem. When businesses believe they have a spending problem, they react by wanting to cut costs, get smaller, and restrict. My job is to help them recognize what they could be doing *more* of and how they can expand. For example, I might suggest they bring on team members with different skills that are relevant to the emerging business market, or I might ask them to sit down with me and reflect on whether they're asking relevant or big enough questions. Perhaps they need to invest in other entrepreneurial relationships, whatever those may be. When they're afraid and lean toward getting small, I remind them to think *big*.

And the same goes for us. It's crucial to recognize that when we allow fear to hold us back, especially the fear of scarcity, we can inadvertently restrict our potential for growth. If we let the fear of taking risks or trying something new consume us, we limit ourselves from embracing opportunities that could lead to greater success and fulfillment. Being afraid is often what causes us to shrink into ourselves, where we become smaller, more insecure, and less willing to grab hold of opportunities when they present themselves. And in those moments, it's important to remember that opportunities are also a resource, and they are abundant. Living in accordance with the belief that things are finite is an inherent flaw of our society, but we can overcome that flaw by recognizing that scarcity only exists within our minds. And if we can change our mindset to one of abundance that embraces the idea of infinite possibilities, we can create a reality for ourselves that is only limited by what we can imagine.

If I haven't already said this, I *love* to travel. Adventure is one of the core values I try to shape my life around, and I have even vowed to visit fifty countries before I turn fifty (at the time of writing this, I have eleven countries left and just six years to go!). On one of my visits to Costa Rica, I found myself in a secluded area, away from all the light pollution of the city. To my amazement, it wasn't even remotely dark. In fact, the sky above me was like an enormous canvas splattered with the most incredible, spectacular stars. I had never seen anything like it before. Looking up at the night sky and the vastness of our galaxy and our infinite universe that expanded above me, I felt a strange wave of comforting insignificance as I took it all in.

Back at home, I had been anxious about so many things: my business, making sure we had enough cash flow, my employees, the economy, politics, and all this stuff that just didn't feel important to me at that moment. Knowing that there was so much out there that was so much bigger than me and my fears was enlightening. Remember that just being alive on this planet, here and now, as you are, is an incredibly spectacular thing. Obstacles and fears are a guaranteed part of success, but the takeaway is to always remember to zoom out and take in the bigger picture. When we do that, we create room for the biggest changes to happen.

✓ CHECK YOURSELF

I don't want to come across like the things that worry you don't matter, because they do. But I want to help you overcome the progress paralysis that often comes with our concerns. So, when you are grappling with limiting beliefs or literal obstacles in your path, remember to zoom out. Consider whether the problem you're currently facing will still have a significant effect on your life five days down the road. What about five months? How about five years? The

continued

sooner we are able to define, accept, and strategize a way around our obstacles, the sooner we can get back on track to our higher purpose.

Daily gratitude

For a lot of my young life, I lived in the fear of scarcity. I was raised with the belief that there was never enough (and sometimes there truly wasn't). I thought I was never enough because of the nature of my relationship with my own father and the men that tried—and failed—to replace him. But it wasn't until I was brave enough to break free from those limiting beliefs and understand that I *was* enough and that there *was* abundance that I realized I had the power to create anything I set my mind to. Now, as an adult, I do everything in my power to fuel that mindset, to keep myself grounded in the belief that not only does abundance exist, but that I already have it.

Years ago, I made the decision to start a small behavior that would have a big impact on how I lived the rest of my life. At the time, I was living in a deep, dark state where I believed that life sucked and nothing good was ever going to happen for me. I told myself I was a victim and had no power over my circumstances, and if I'm being honest, I just got under my own skin. One day I decided that, instead of focusing on all the obstacles and fears that cluttered the path in front of me, I was going to start making an effort to look for miracles around me, and start being grateful for my place on earth.

From that day on, I made a promise to write down five *unique* things I was grateful for every single day, and over years of doing this, this pattern has turned into what I like to call my gratitude journal. If you're stuck on what to do to start changing your own life, I can honestly say that practicing daily gratitude has had a positive impact on my life. Now, I can look back on a random day from a previous year and enjoy those moments all over again.

On the days when it is difficult to find five things, I force myself to focus until I find five things to be grateful for. Remember, they don't always have to be big, extravagant things. Sometimes the simplest moments are enough to be grateful for. As such tiny humans who kick around in a giant, immeasurable universe, we can often feel overwhelmed. Our minds are small compared to the abundance that exists out there, and that's why it can be easy to crowd our mind with thoughts of scarcity. *However*, if we can harness our ability to ground ourselves and fill our minds with gratitude, there won't be any space left to hold on to any of the fears and worries that are holding us back.

A year from today, you won't even remember the things you were feeling overwhelmed by, and if you commit to practicing gratitude and savoring the good things, guess what? You will fill your mind with an abundance of good things, and when you hold them in your mind, you will manifest more abundance into your reality going forward.

Window of opportunity

At the beginning of this book, I introduced you to a version of myself that was at rock bottom, the lowest point on earth, both literally and emotionally. It seems only fitting then to bookend that story by sharing with you where I found myself a little over two years later. My wife and I decided to pick a theme to try and encapsulate the coming year together. The theme we chose was *light*. With that theme in mind, we tried to do anything and everything that we could involving light. From catching the lights of Las Vegas to enjoying a candlelit instrumental concert featuring the music of Taylor Swift, we were there for all of it. And of course, at the top of our list of things we wanted to do to honor that year's theme: seeing the northern lights.

If you haven't heard of them, or don't know exactly what causes them, the northern lights (also known as the aurora borealis) are an almost supernatural-looking phenomenon caused by light particles from the sun that get trapped in Earth's magnetic field and interact with some of the gases in our atmosphere to create brilliant colors that dance across the night sky.

We knew they were something to marvel at, but the chances of seeing the northern lights during the months they are visible are as little as 3 percent. Nevertheless, we packed our bags and flew from Denver to London, then from London to Stockholm. From there, we flew to Helsinki to catch another flight to Pyhä, Finland, where we drove for almost two hours across icy roads until we finally got to the cabin where we would be staying. All in all, it took us longer to get there than the length of our whole trip, but we knew it would be worth it if it meant we'd be able to witness something so spectacular.

Unfortunately, the weather had other plans in store for us. The first night was a total whiteout: a snowstorm that wouldn't let up until morning. Once the snowstorm finally was over, my wife and I decided we would venture out into the cold, crisp air for a walk.

As we meandered around, getting familiar with the area, we stumbled across a quaint little tourism shop and popped inside to ask them if they could help us schedule a dog sled tour for ourselves. While we were chatting, in true Steve fashion, I went to work asking them as many questions as I could—in particular, if they had any insights on when or if the northern lights would be visible. To our disappointment, the workers informed us that it had been almost a week since they'd seen the aurora, and they expected it to be at least a few more days until the phenomenon would be visible again. I could have left it at that and accepted that we probably weren't going to see them, but I persisted with more questions about their neighborhood and what it was like to live and work in such a marvelous part of the world.

Based on what happened next, I can only assume that they took well to all of my inquisitiveness. I obviously don't want to take all the credit here, but if I hadn't been curious and determined enough to ask questions, my wife and I never would have gotten their recommendation.

They suggested that we install a special aurora app the locals used to alert them that the northern lights were going to be visible. We thanked them for their help booking our tour and for giving us the inside scoop on the app, and left, feeling like the possibility of seeing the aurora was smaller than ever.

Back at the cabin, we cranked up the heat, gathered some snacks, and sat in the living room, playing games and enjoying each other's company. I was grateful to have this time with my wife, but I also was struggling to subdue the feeling of disappointment. I was totally bummed that we weren't going to get to see what we came for, and it felt like our whole trip had been in vain. I tried to talk myself through how to let things go, and I reminded myself that regardless of whether we ended up seeing the lights or not, there was already an abundance of things to be grateful for on this trip with each other.

There are many steps we can take to let things go, but saying a quiet prayer is what works for me. So I did that. I said that it was important for us to get to see the northern lights as a couple if it was at all possible, but that whatever the outcome would be, I would accept that and be okay with it. The weather had been miserable and overcast all day, so I reminded myself that I wouldn't be disappointed if it didn't happen, because what I was asking for was a miracle. I let go of my desire, and we went back to playing our game together.

It couldn't have been more than twenty minutes later when my phone buzzed with the sound of a notification. I checked it, and lo and behold, it was the aurora app. I jumped to my feet and hurried to open the app. The built-in visibility scale was showing that there was a level-two visibility of the northern lights, so we rushed into our room, which was fitted with a glass ceiling and huddled together on the bed, craning our necks to squint up at the sky, but I couldn't see anything.

"Do you see anything?" I whispered, as if speaking too loudly would scare the lights away. My wife shook her head.

Disappointed, we returned to our game in the living room. We were *so close*, but the marvelous masterpiece had eluded us. I set my phone back down, and again I reminded myself that being able to share this time together with my wife, who's my best friend, was priceless and being able to visit a foreign country with her (and check another one off of my fifty before fifty bucket list) was in and of itself a fulfilling experience.

I was truly happy, and I had so much to be grateful for. We took turns drawing cards and picking up chips, and then it was my turn to play. I reached for a card and gathered my chips and then . . . *buzz!* Another notification from the app, and hesitantly, I checked it.

"The auroras are at a level five!" I exclaimed.

Filled with sheer delight, we sprang to our feet and once again rushed to our bed under its ceiling of glass. We shut off all the lights and huddled together again to peer up at the windows. The sky was still swathed with clouds, and I felt my heart drop.

What's with all the false hope? I thought.

But then, something truly remarkable happened. The clouds above our window parted, revealing the most spectacular sight I've ever seen in my life. The sky was suddenly crystal clear, and the auroras were in full swing. For the next fifteen minutes, the sky was lit up with dozens of green and teal electromagnetic flares, exploding against the most breathtaking backdrop of stars.

I wondered if, just maybe, we could find a place somewhere secluded just outside of town where there weren't other lights that might interfere with our visibility. I decided I would warm up the car and told my wife to put on her warmest clothes and meet me out front. We drove a few miles in the general direction of *away* to see if we could get a better view, but by the time we had found a spot, the clouds had circled back over.

The next day, the skies were clearer than they'd been on our entire trip. The clouds were gone, but unfortunately, so were the northern lights. We flew home, and it was another five days before my phone buzzed again, this time while I was in a meeting all the way across the world in Colorado, saying that the auroras were back and in full visibility. It just goes to show you that the window of opportunity for something might be brief, so when it happens, you have to act on it. I'm sharing this story with you in the hopes that you will recognize the way it encapsulates everything we've been talking about.

Bottom to the top

A life of abundance looks different for everyone, but creating a truly abundant life is shaped by working on a few core elements. Like any good thing, it's a process that takes time, commitment, and tenacity, but with a positive mindset and the right plan of action, you'll be able to create a life of abundance for yourself. No matter which way you acquire them, the cornerstones of abundance are faith, hard work, resilience, gratitude, and self-fulfillment.

First and foremost, have faith. It doesn't need to be founded in religion, but believe and expect that good things will happen and be willing to receive them.

Second, do the hard work. Put in all the effort you can muster. I could have easily just downloaded a video of the northern lights to watch, but I didn't. I set the goal of going to see them in person, I got my wife motivated to travel, and we put in the work together. We didn't just manifest; we planned, strategized, and executed.

Third, when you put questions out into the Universe, be willing to accept no for an answer and reframe whatever doesn't satisfy you. Teach yourself to know when to progress and when to pivot. Recognize when the desire for something becomes the obstacle in your path and understand how letting go of that desire can open you up to receiving it.

Fourth, learn to look for miracles and allow them to guide you as you practice gratitude ahead of anything else. To me, the northern lights are a miracle. Yes, I know technically they are a scientific phenomenon, but when you think about it, those lights would continue to shine over this planet whether we were here to witness it or not. Humans are not the be-all and end-all of existence, and this planet would keep turning even if we weren't here. So, have gratitude for the marvelous things and don't take it personally when they don't happen. We may not have had that experience, but in its place, we were given an opportunity to learn patience and maybe to receive something greater somewhere down the line.

Finally, get to know yourself. Dig deep to find what drives you, what matters to you, and what your purpose is. Once you know that, go and do the work, build the skills, and do the hard things and the scary things. Find your limits and push them. Be uncomfortable, grind, and see how far your ambitions will take you. And when you come home at the end of the day, remember to give time to the people who support you.

The higher power that exists out there in the universe is very aware of us. It is very aware of *you*. I believe there are no coincidences and we are here on earth to fulfill our purpose and know that we will be blessed along the way. No matter what is important to us, if we act with good intentions and a tenacious sense of dedication, abundance is waiting out there for us. Don't let yourself be confined to fear and scarcity, because these are superficial limits created by your mind. Get out of your head. There is abundance out there.

When I manifested and asked God for the chance to see the northern lights, it's not like the whole world stopped. In fact, I'm certain thousands of people all around the world also received things they were asking for and working for. I went from the lowest place on earth, being down, looking down, and feeling down. But I ended up in a great, high-up space, where I felt entirely uplifted and rejuvenated. When I was in Finland, way up in the mountains, my spirits were raised, and I had plenty of gratitude. The man I was when I was at the lowest place on earth is gone now. Looking up at the sky and out at the abundance that exists in the world around me and in the universe beyond, I am a changed man. If you're in a low place now, know that it isn't permanent. Change is possible. It is uncomfortable and scary, but if you set your mind to where you want to go and don't stop until you get there, you will never fail.

When I set out to write this book, my greatest hope was to create a practical guide that would empower people to build a successful life for themselves, both financially and beyond. The tools and strategies, along with the practical, psychological, and philosophical calls to action that were interspersed in our conversation outline the exact same framework I used to totally transform my personal and professional life into one of abundance. I needed to completely reform my mindset, dig deep, and get honest with myself about what my values were and how to create a life that would honor those values.

I also had to overcome obstacles and learn to let go of my desires in order to receive the things I wanted. From a business perspective, I had to teach myself to be financially literate and learn how to strategize and set goals that would help me create the life I'd envisioned. And when I realized that those things didn't completely fulfill me, I had to embark on an entirely different journey of self-discovery, starting with realigning my life according to my priorities. I had to recognize that my purpose in life was less about fulfilling myself and more about helping others find true fulfillment. I learned that there was indeed some truth behind the laws of attraction and vibration, but that those things don't mean much without putting in the hard work. I learned to recognize that there is immeasurable value in giving to others, even if it means giving time when you cannot give money, and I grew to understand the importance of creating space in myself to be open to receiving from others (truth be told, I'm still working on this one).

I know that no two people walk the same path in life and that one person's idea of thriving may not be the same for someone else, but through my experiences as a financial enthusiast, chief financial officer, and businessman, I've learned that success isn't defined by the number of valuable things you accumulate over your lifetime—it's about creating a life that honors the things you value. If you attempt to define your success by your financial goals, you will end up feeling empty and unsatisfied. Yes, money can resolve immediate difficulties, but it cannot fulfill you. So, go after what you want when it comes to being financially fit, create a business, and perhaps another one, but remember to nurture the more human parts of life as well.

I realize I've spent a lot of this book trying to teach you what I know about financial literacy and the importance of building daily patterns centered around the six factors of the financial fitness model. Without a doubt, that knowledge and those principles are *essential* to becoming financially free, but my hope is that you recognize that financial freedom is not where your journey ends but where your life truly begins. You should be zealous and fearless as you pursue the life you want, but also remember to be gentle and compassionate with those with whom you choose to share your life. I want you to not only be able to identify these tools but truly take advantage of them as you apply them to your professional and personal circumstances.

My path to success wasn't a straightforward one, and I failed many times along the way, but my hope is that through sharing my story with you and the skills and knowledge I learned along the way, you will be empowered to act in ways that truly fulfill you and inspired to create a life of abundance for yourself.

Exercise Your Knowledge

For our last activity, I'd like to invite you to reflect on what you have learned over the course of reading this book and think about how you can apply some of the core concepts to your own life, starting today. Feel free to write down your answers, or just spend a few minutes in quiet reflection on each.

1. *Defining your abundance.* Take a moment to envision a life of abundance that resonates with your deepest values. What does a life overflowing with fulfillment and prosperity look like to you?

2. *Having faith in your unique abilities.* Reflect on the power of faith and belief in shaping your journey toward abundance. How can you cultivate

faith in yourself and the possibility of good things happening?

3. *Embracing change.* Explore the idea of embracing change and being open to new possibilities. How can you gracefully accept a no and reframe obstacles as stepping stones toward growth? Reflect on the desires that may no longer serve you and be willing to release them. How can you welcome change as a catalyst for transformation?

4. *Being grounded in gratitude.* What are the wonders of life that you appreciate the most? How can you create more space for gratitude in your daily routine and give time to small things that bring you immense joy?

5. *Discovering yourself.* What drives you from within? How can you align your actions with your core values so you are living in harmony with your purpose? How can you become more comfortable stepping beyond your comfort zone and nurturing your ambitions?

As you reflect, remember that the path to abundance is not just about the finances—it's about discovering your true values, aligning your actions with your dreams, and embracing the abundance that surrounds you. With this newfound knowledge and reinvigoration, may you embark on a journey of prosperity and create a life filled with purpose, joy, and fulfillment.

Notes

Chapter 1

1. Hannah Ritchie, Max Roser, and Pablo Rosado, "Energy," OurWorldInData.org., 2022, retrieved from https://ourworldindata.org/energy.
2. "Average Income around the World," Worlddata.info, n.d., https://www.worlddata.info/average-income.php.
3. John Rawls, *A Theory of Justice*, rev. ed. (Cambridge, MA: Belknap Press, 1999).
4. "Average Income around the World," Worlddata.info.

Chapter 2

1. Daniel Kahneman and Angus Deaton, "High Income Improves Evaluation of Life but Not Emotional Well-Being," *Proceedings of the National Academy of Sciences* 107, no. 38 (2010), https://doi.org/10.1073/pnas.1011492107.

Chapter 3

1. Prentice Mulford, *Thoughts Are Things* (New York: Harper & Brothers, 1889).

Chapter 5

1. *Oprah Presents Master Class*, season 1, episode 8, April 2, 2011, video, 10:09, featuring Oprah Winfrey discussing how she got a part in *The Color Purple*, https://www.youtube.com/watch?v=Vpw7crMrA6o&ab_channel=SoulFoodLifestyle.

Chapter 7

1. U.S. Census Bureau, "About 13.1 Percent Have a Master's, Professional Degree or Doctorate," Census.gov, October 8, 2021, https://www.census.gov/library/stories/2019/02/number-of-people-with-masters-and-phd-degrees-double-since-2000.html.

2. Tony Robbins, "'How to Follow Through/Persist with Your Goals," JayZed, YouTube, February 5, 2010, video, 10:04, https://www.youtube.com/watch?v=4faufiXA7Bw.

Chapter 10

1. "Statistics Archive—The Money Charity," https://themoneycharity.org.uk/money-statistics.

2. Lane Gillespie, "Average American Debt Statistics," *Bankrate*, January 13, 2023, https://www.bankrate.com/personal-finance/debt/average-american-debt/.

3. Tim Maxwell, "3 Reasons to Pay More Than the Minimum on Your Credit Card," *Experian*, May 12, 2023, https://www.experian.com/blogs/ask-experian/3-reasons-to-pay-more-than-the-minimum-on-your-credit-card/#:~:text=Paying%20more%20than%20the%20minimum,and%20pay%20off%20debt%20earlier.

4. "Apple Inc. Will Provide Full Customer Refunds of at Least $32.5 Million to Settle FTC Complaint It Charged for Kids' In-App Purchases Without Parental Consent," Federal Trade Commission (press release), January 15, 2014, https://www.ftc.gov/news-events/news/press-releases/2014/01/apple-inc-will-provide-full-consumer-refunds-least-325-million-settle-ftc-complaint-it-charged-kids.

5. Soomin Ryu and Lu Fan, "The Relationship between Financial Worries and Psychological Distress among U.S. Adults," *Journal of Family* and *Economic Issues* 44, no. 1 (February 1, 2022): 16–33, https://doi.org/10.1007/s10834-022-09820-9.

Chapter 11

1. Sarah O'Brien, "Lack of Financial Literacy Cost 15% of Adults at Least $10,000 in 2022. Here's How the Rest Fared," *CNBC*, January 19, 2023, https://www.cnbc.com/2023/01/19/heres-how-much-people-say-lack-of-financial-literacy-cost-in-2022.html.

Chapter 12

1. Bronnie Ware, *The Top Five Regrets of the Dying: A Life Transformed by the Dearly Departing* (Brighton-Le-Sands NSW: Hay House, 2019).

Chapter 13

1. Tal Yarkoni, Yoni K. Ashar, and Tor D. Wager, "Interactions between Donor Agreeableness and Recipient Characteristics in Predicting Charitable Donation and Positive Social Evaluation," *PeerJ* 3 (August 18, 2015): e1089, https://doi.org/10.7717/peerj.1089.

2. "Third Time Isn't Always the Charm: Divorce More Likely after Second and Third Marriages," Meriwether & Tharp LLC (blog), n.d., https://mtlawoffice.com/news/third-time-isnt-always-the-charm-divorce-more-likely-after-second-and-third-marriages.

3. August McLaughlin, "7 Money Issues That Can Lead to Divorce," *GOBankingRates*, March 21, 2022, https://www.gobankingrates.com/saving-money/relationships/blame-money-reasons-marriages-fail/.

4. "BECU Survey Discovers Majority of Parents Aren't Talking with Kids about Money," *Cision*, October 3, 2019, https://www.prnewswire.com/news-releases/becu-survey-discovers-majority-of-parents-arent-talking-with-kids-about-money-300930307.html.

5. "BECU Survey."

6. Leora Klapper, Annamaria Lusardi, and Peter van Oudheusden, "Financial Literacy around the World," Standard & Poor's Ratings Services Global Financial Literacy Survey, 2015, https://gflec.org/wp-content/uploads/2015/11/Finlit_paper_16_F2_singles.pdf.

7. Ying Lin, Julian Mutz, Peter Clough, and Kostas A. Papageorgiou, "Mental Toughness and Individual Differences in Learning, Educational and Work Performance, Psychological Well-Being, and Personality: A Systematic Review," *Frontiers in Psychology* 8 (August 11, 2017), https://doi.org/10.3389/fpsyg.2017.01345.

8. Yilan Xu, Daniel A. Briley, Jeffrey R. Brown, and Brent W. Roberts, "Genetic and Environmental Influences on Household Financial Distress," *Journal of Economic Behavior and Organization* 142 (October 1, 2017): 404–24, https://doi.org/10.1016/j.jebo.2017.08.001.

9. Mary Fennell, "Elderly Hispanics More Likely to Reside in Poor-Quality Nursing Homes," *Health Affairs* 29, no. 1 (January 1, 2010): 65–73, https://doi.org/10.1377/hlthaff.2009.0003.

Chapter 14

1. David Mead and Simon Sinek, *Find Your Why: A Practical Guide for Discovering Purpose for You and Your Team* (New York: Portfolio Penguin, 2017), https://openlibrary.org/books/OL26397565M/Find_Your_Why.

Chapter 15

1. *Science World Report*, "Plants Physically React to Leaf Vibrations Caused by Hungry Caterpillars," July 2, 2014, video, https://www.scienceworldreport.com/articles/15785/20140702/plants-physically-react-leaf-vibrations-caused-hungry-caterpillars-video.htm.

2. King's College London, "Do Negative Thoughts Increase Risk of Alzheimer's Disease?" *Medical Press*, November 17, 2014, https://medicalxpress.com/news/2014-11-negative-thoughts-alzheimer-disease.html.

3. David R. Hawkins, *Power vs. Force: The Hidden Determinants of Human Behavior* (Carlsbad, CA: Hay House, 2002).

Chapter 17

1. Rubina Kapil, "How and Why to Practice Self-Care," Mental Health First Aid (News & Updates), March 14, 2022, https://www.mentalhealthfirstaid.org/2022/03/how-and-why-to-practice-self-care/.

2. Kevin Ashton, *How to Fly a Horse: The Secret History of Creation, Invention, and Discovery* (New York: Anchor Books, 2015).

3. "Train Your Brain," Harvard Health (blog), February 15, 2021, https://www.health.harvard.edu/mind-and-mood/train-your-brain.

About the Author

A uthor, business leader, and podcast host Steve Coughran has over two decades of experience driving business excellence. He is the founder of Coltivar, a consulting firm that empowers companies to drive successful financial, operational, and strategic transformations. Beyond growing and managing Coltivar from the ground up, he has been a strategic CFO, management consultant, and entrepreneur, gaining experience in accelerating growth of SaaS businesses, engaging in mergers and acquisitions, delivering corporate restructurings and turnarounds, raising debt and equity capital, and building high-performing teams by connecting with people on an emotional level.

In addition to *Reframing Rich*, Steve is the author of two previous books, *Outsizing* and *Delivering Value*, in which he compiles relevant research and his years of professional experience to provide readers with the keys to unlocking strategic growth for their companies. Steve hosts multiple podcasts, including *Boosting Your Financial IQ, Strategic Financial Leadership, Business Strategy*, and *Finance with Kids*, where he shares his knowledge of strategy and finance with others and provides listeners with a range of personal and professional financial advice.

Beyond his role as a turnaround expert, Steve is a staunch advocate for financial literacy and seeks to make the world a better, more prosperous place by inspiring leaders to build better businesses so they can create abundance and raise the quality of life in their communities. He believes the best way to fight poverty is to help foster market-creating innovation and business growth on a grassroots level.

Steve is a CPA, earned his MBA from the Fuqua School of Business at Duke University, and studied international business across four continents. He advanced his specialization in strategy through study at the Executive Education Program at the Tuck School of Business at Dartmouth College. Steve lives with his wife and children in Denver, Colorado. When he's not working, he enjoys running, traveling around the world, and asking questions.

www.ingramcontent.com/pod-product-compliance
Lightning Source LLC
Chambersburg PA
CBHW030458210326
41597CB00013B/722